A HERITAGE OF SHIPS

All over the British Isles there are maritime museums where ships, their sailing days over, are lovingly restored and put on show to the public. Some, like Nelson's flagship HMS *Victory* and Captain Scott's RRS *Discovery*, are famous historically; others, like the clipper *Cutty Sark*, have acquired a fame of their own; all are fascinating to visit.

There could be no better guide to the ship museums of the United Kingdom than Alexander McKee—a naval historian and the man whose labours over twenty years led to the raising of the *Mary Rose* in 1982. With insight and knowledge he leads us over great warships and clippers, over steam packets, lifeboats and canal barges, describing where and how they were built, their careers afloat and their story in retirement. From Dundee to Ramsgate, from Portsmouth to Bristol and Cardiff, from Liverpool to the Isle of Man and Belfast, he takes us on a tour of Britain's maritime history in war and peace.

More than twenty museums are covered in detail, with information about opening times, admission fees and how to get there, and each chapter is illustrated with a wealth of unusual photographs, largely taken by the author, showing aspects of the ships that the ordinary visitor might easily miss. At the end of the book is a complete list of all ship museums in the British Isles, including those not covered in the main text.

All of us have a ship museum within reasonable distance of where we live. This absorbing guide will awaken an interest that could become a lifelong hobby.

ALEXANDER McKEE grew up with the sea in his blood. As the son of a naval surgeon, he was familiar with ships throughout his boyhood, and he has spent much of his adult life sailing, swimming and diving in the waters of Britain and the Mediterranean. Among the twenty or so books he has published are many about ships and the sea, including, most recently, *How We Found the Mary Rose, Tarquin's Ship: The Etruscan Wreck in Campese Bay*, and new editions of *The Golden Wreck: The Tragedy of the Royal Charter* and *From Merciless Invaders: The Defeat of the Spanish Armada*.

A HERITAGE OF SHIPS

A Regional Guide

ALEXANDER MCKEE

SOUVENIR PRESS

First published 1988 by Souvenir Press Ltd,
43 Great Russell Street, London WC1B 3PA
and simultaneously in Canada

ISBN 0 285 628550

Photoset, printed and bound in Great Britain by
WBC Bristol and Maesteg

CONTENTS

ACKNOWLEDGEMENTS

The author would like to thank the following for their help in compiling this book:

Vice-Admiral Sir Patrick Bayly, KBE, CB, DSC, Director of the Maritime Trust, for much documentation and background.

Ilse McKee, for assistance with photography of *Alliance, Holland I, Belfast, Cutty Sark, Foudroyant, Great Britain, Mary Rose, Victory, Warrior* and Exeter Maritime Museum.

Booklets, documentation and/or illustrations were supplied by: For HMS *Alliance*: RN Submarine Museum, Gosport; for HMS *Belfast*: Imperial War Museum, London; for HMS *Caroline*: Lt-Cdr M. Ratcliffe, RN, Ulster Division RNR, Belfast; for HMS *Cavalier*: Colin Douglas of AMARC (Assorted Maritime and Related Charities) and *Brighton Evening Argus*; for clipper *Cutty Sark*: Capt. F. Bell, The 'Cutty Sark' Society, Greenwich; for RRS *Discovery*: Jonathan Bryant, Chief Executive, A NATION'S ENTERPRISE: The Spirit of Dundee; for TS *Foudroyant*: HMS Foudroyant Trust; and Society for Nautical Research, including several informal visits; for HMS *Gannet*: Leisure Services Department, Gosport; The Gosport Society; David Muffett; for SS *Great Britain*: B.H. Wheddon, Commercial Director, SS Great Britain Trading Ltd, Bristol; for *Mary Rose*: Arthur Rogers, Director of Fund Raising and Public Relations, Mary Rose Trust (especially for Naval Base layout and visitor information, and for use of the Trust trade mark); Mike Taylor for Trust photos; and Shell UK Ltd; for yacht *Peggy*: Ms Y.M. Hayhurst, Assistant Keeper, The Manx Museum and National Trust, Isle of Man; for schooner *Result*: Michael McCaughan, Maritime Historian, Ulster Folk and Transport Museum; for yacht *Sundowner*: Robert B. Matkin, Chairman, East Kent Maritime Trust, Ramsgate; for launch *Turbinia*: J.M. Twelves, Senior Museums Officer (Commercial Activities), Tyne and Wear Museums Service, Newcastle-upon-Tyne; for HMS *Unicorn*: Cdr J.A. Smith, FAAI, RN, Development Manager, The Unicorn Preservation Society; for HMS *Victory*: Lt-Cdr Peter Whitlock, RN, a former captain of HMS *Victory*, especially for his booklet *Nelson and Victory*, the best of its kind I know (I bought my first about 1930); for HMS *Warrior*:

Ian Robinson, Marketing and Publicity Officer, HMS Warrior 1860 (including an early invitation to see over the ship before it officially opened to the public); for The Boat Museum, Ellesmere Port: Tony Hirst, Director; for the Welsh Industrial and Maritime Museum, Cardiff: Dr David Jenkins, Research Assistant; the Scottish Maritime Museum, Irvine.

Finally, all our thanks are due to the original divers on the *Mary Rose*, without whose perseverance she would not have been raised; without that example the *Warrior* might not have come to Portsmouth, and there would have been no unique historic ships complex in Great Britain, exceeding anything to be seen anywhere else in the world.

Alexander McKee

PREFACE

After Salamis, where in 480 BC the Greeks utterly defeated a massive Persian fleet in a battle decisive for Western civilisation, three captured triremes were dragged ashore and consecrated as monuments to victory—one on the Isthmus overlooking the waters where the battle had taken place, one by the sea-temple of Sunium, and one on the island of Salamis itself. Some forty years afterwards, the Greek 'father of history', Herodotus, born 484, saw the war galley preserved above the Isthmus. There is no sign of it now, although the tomb of the victor, Themistocles, has been discovered—but only belatedly recognised, after the remains had been discarded.

After Francis Drake's circumnavigation of the world between 1577 and 1580, which brought an immense revenue of Spanish gold, silver and jewels to a penurious English Crown, as well as great national glory, Queen Elizabeth proposed that Drake's flagship *Golden Hind* should be preserved in a specially built dock near Deptford on the Thames, which would be roofed over to prevent her decaying. The scheme got as far as an estimate—the building of a brick wall 180 feet long and 15 feet high for £130, and the construction of a timber-and-tile roof at a further cost of £90.

Possibly the threat from Spain, culminating in the arrival in the Channel of the Spanish Armada in 1588, prevented the memorial hall being built. Nevertheless, the *Golden Hind* attracted visitors, including foreigners. Thomas Platter, a Swiss, went to see her in 1599 but thought her fabric so rotten that he was tempted to take a souvenir home to Basel. A Dutch chart of about 1601–6, Wagher's *Thresoor de Zeerart* published by Benjamin Wright, included a sketch of a vessel lying ashore at Deptford with the note 'Captain Dracke's Schip'. In 1618, nearly 40 years after she had been laid up, the Secretary to the Venetian Ambassador wrote: 'We likewise passed along the banks of the Thames in sight of some relics of the ship of the famous Captain Drake, which looked exactly like the bleached ribs and bare skull of a dead horse.' In about 1662, after more than 80 years of neglect, by breaking or by burning, or both, the site was tidied up. Some of the *Golden Hind's* timber was used to make furniture for academic institutions—a chair for the Bodleian

Library in Oxford and a table for Middle Temple Hall in London. Drake's achievement remains, but his ship has vanished.

Nevertheless, at intervals aggrieved citizens write to the Portsmouth *News* to protest about being charged to see the *Mary Rose* or HMS *Victory*, assuming (incorrectly) that they themselves paid vast sums for the raising of the former, and that old sailing ships, unlike houses and motor cars, either require no upkeep or have it supplied free, like the winds.

The triremes of Salamis, Drake's round-the-globe ship, and Nelson's *Victory* were proclamations of national pride. In the same category are the two United States frigates, *Constellation* and *Constitution*, victors over British frigates; in Norway, Amundsen's Polar ship the *Fram*; and in the Soviet Union the cruiser *Aurora*, symbol of the October Revolution. There are many others.

The Viking longships excavated from burial mounds—for they were the tombs of chiefs and may be ceremonial vessels—and their display as impressive artefacts of the Scandinavian past in a purpose-built museum near Oslo in Norway, must represent a more scholarly approach. A similar historical drive lay behind the deliberate discovery followed by recovery of the Swedish galleon *Wasa* from the depths of Stockholm harbour in 1961, and of Henry VIII's carrack *Mary Rose* from Spithead in 1982. In both these cases much of the contents of the ships at the time of sinking were recovered also—indisputably genuine.

In a different category, not represented in this book, are the various 'replicas'—from Viking craft to classical triremes—built to test a theory; as arguments in timber they may be valid, even useful. Commerce and the 'heritage' industry have introduced another category of historic ship—the fake. Although these do not feature in the following pages, they may serve some useful purpose in enabling the twentieth century to visualise its past. And so rapid has technical progress become that many twentieth-century ships are, with reason, being preserved as relics of a time that has vanished. Some of these recent ships and vessels I have included.

Alexander McKee
Hayling Island, Hampshire,
November 1987.

1 *PORTSMOUTH NAVAL BASE*

All enquiries on group visits should be addressed to the Bookings and Information Office, Portsmouth Naval Heritage Trust, Building 1/24, College Road, HM Naval Base, Portsmouth, PO1 3LX. Telephone: (0705) 839766.

How to Get There
By road: via the A3(M) from London or M27 from Southampton and Brighton, then following the signposted route via the M275 into Portsmouth. There is no car or coach access to the Naval Base. (See map for car parks and coach facilities.) By rail: to Portsmouth Harbour Station, part of the Hard Transport Interchange. By ferry: from Gosport or the Isle of Wight.

The Royal Naval Museum
The museum stands alongside HMS *Victory* in the heart of the Naval Base. Housed in three graceful Georgian storehouses, it covers the entire history of the Royal Navy from Tudor times to the South Atlantic Campaign in 1982.

Opening Times
For the individual ships, see following pages. For the museum: Every day 10.30 am to 5.00 pm. Closed for one week at Christmas. Last tickets sold 30 minutes before closing.

Entrance Fees
See following pages for admission fees to the ships. For the museum: Adults 75p, OAPs and children 5 to 16 50p (60p and 40p respectively when combined with a ship visit.
Group rates ten per cent discount.

PORTSMOUTH NAVAL BASE

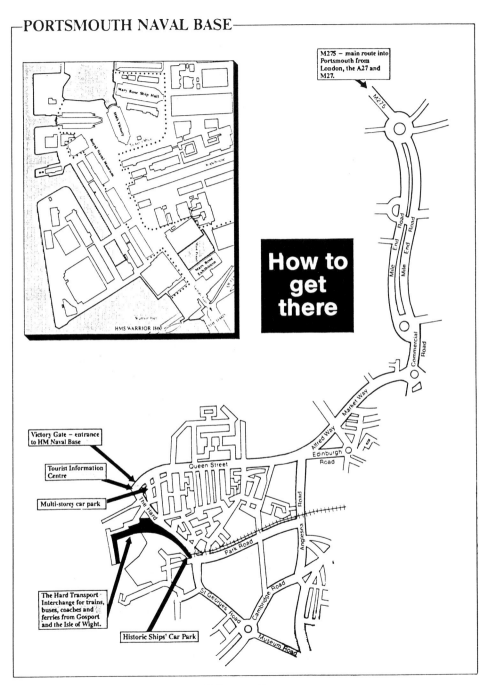

Reproduced courtesy Portsmouth Naval Heritage Trust

HMS *Victory*: Nelson's Flagship

HISTORY

Built (for £57,748) at Chatham	1759-65
Commissioned	1778
Major refit	1801-3
Severe battle damage, Trafalgar	1805
Paid off to reserve	1812
Moved to present dry dock	1922

SPECIFICATIONS

Length, figurehead to taffrail	69m (226 ft 6 ins)
Length of gundeck	56.5m (186 ft)
Length of keel	46.5m (152 ft 3 ins)
Extreme beam	16m (51 ft 10 ins)
Depth of hold	6.5m (21 ft 6 ins)
Tonnage	2,162 tons
Tonnage (Displacement)	3,500 tons
Complement at Trafalgar	850 officers and men

ARMAMENT

lower gundeck	30 32-pdrs
middle gundeck	28 24-pdrs
upper gundeck	30 12-pounders
quarterdeck	12 12-pdrs
forecastle	2 12-pdrs and
	2 68-pdr carronades

During the Napoleonic wars there were four sizes of warship considered fit to lie in the line of battle and engage the main body of the enemy. These were the 1st, 2nd, 3rd and 4th Rates. Alternatively they were listed by the nominal number of guns they carried—100, 90, 64-74, 50. The *Victory* was a 1st Rate, carrying, at the time of Trafalgar, 104 guns mostly on the three continuous gundecks. For this reason, the type were sometimes known as three-deckers, dwarfing the two-decker 74s which formed the bulk of the fleets; they were giant headquarters ships for an Admiral and his staff.

HMS *Victory* in the 1950s. *Photo: Alexander McKee*

From the beginning, the *Victory* showed exceptional sailing qualities, handling almost like a two-decker.

But for 13 years after being launched, she remained in the Medway, because these were years of peace. She went to war for the first time in 1778, when the French backed the rebellious American colonists, as the flagship of Admiral Keppel at Portsmouth, and was involved in an indecisive action off Ushant. In 1782, as flagship of Lord Howe, the *Victory* served at the relief of Gibraltar, closely invested by the Spaniards, and fought in the battle of Cape Spartel.

For ten years after that there was peace, until in 1793 began a new round of wars against France, now a revolutionary republic. The *Victory*'s principal war station became the Mediterranean, including the capture of Toulon and the siege of Calvi in Corsica, under Lord Hood, and an indecisive action off Hyeres in 1795. Battles fought between fleets of broadside-gunned ships sailing in line ahead, follow-my-leader style, often were indecisive, but when in the same year Admiral Sir John Jervis took command, with his flag in the *Victory*, there followed in 1797 the timely triumph off Cape St Vincent, in which Commodore Horatio Nelson played a decisive part by breaking off from the formal line-of-battle and disrupting the Spanish line with his own ship, HMS *Captain*.

For the next three years the *Victory* served as hospital ship for the prison hulks at Chatham. Then in 1801 there began a three-year refit which amounted almost to a rebuild, and changes to her appearance similar to those existing today.

The principal duty of the English fleet in this war was to blockade the enemy's ports, which meant keeping the seas at all seasons and in all weathers, which was hard on the ships and harder still on the men who lived in damp, confined spaces without heating and on food and drink long in cask, and yet had to carry out hard physical labour on deck or aloft. A successful commander was one who was able to keep his crews fit and healthy, with high morale, in the most daunting or dismal circumstances. Nelson paid particular attention to detail, for instance making sure that the men working aloft had stormcoats giving sufficient protection.

Nelson, now an Admiral and ennobled, took HMS *Victory* as his flagship in 1803. There followed the 18 months-long blockade of Toulon, the escape of the French Admiral Villeneuve, and a long, unsuccessful chase across the Atlantic to the West Indies and back; Villeneuve slipped into Cadiz to join his Spanish allies, forming a combined fleet greater than that of the English waiting outside, and Nelson returned to England for the last time.

In September 1805, Nelson left Portsmouth in the *Victory* to join his fleet blockading the French and Spanish ships in Cadiz. Napoleon's latest orders to Villeneuve were to get out of port and into the Mediterranean; the invasion of England had been abandoned. But Bonaparte had sacrificed his navy to his army. Although the combined fleet numbered 33 battleships to Nelson's 27, the English fleet was the more effective force, and must win if Nelson could bring on a close action, bringing superior numbers to bear at the point of attack, instead of forming one long line. On 21 October, a day of calm or light winds, and a steadily upheaving swell, the battle of Trafalgar began.

Victory's muster roll shows that she was under strength (not at all unusual then or later) at 819 officers, seamen, marines and servants. About a third of the men were volunteers, and more than half the crew were English; but there were 70 Scots and about the same number of Irish, and some Welsh; and 71 foreigners, including more than 20 Americans and three Frenchmen (the latter probably refugees). Their average age was 25 (on the high side), but only a tenth were over 40; the youngest was a Scots lad of ten years.

By sunset, Villeneuve was a prisoner, Nelson was dead. The *Victory* was a wreck, but no English ship had sunk or surrendered. Eighteen French and Spanish ships lay disabled in the battle area, one of them on fire; 13 had British prize crews aboard. It was a very

One of Victory's gun decks.
Photo: Alexander McKee

Down in the hold.
Photo: Alexander McKee

total victory, typical of Nelson; but very hard won, for the enemy had fought with great bravery.

After returning to Portsmouth under jury rig, the *Victory* was refitted at Chatham, reduced to a 2nd Rate. In 1808 she served in the Baltic against the Russians as flagship of Admiral Saumarez; in 1809 she helped evacuate Sir John Moore's troops 'Dunkirked' by Bonaparte at Corunna, and in January 1811 transported infantry reinforcements to Sir Arthur Wellesley (later Duke of Wellington). In 1812 she ended her sea-going career, performing various harbour duties in Portsmouth for more than a century afterwards. It was while moored in the harbour in 1903 that the *Victory* suffered really serious damage—the runaway ironclad *Neptune* collided with the old wooden wall and nearly sank her.

By 1921 something had to be done to prevent her from going to the breakers, and the task was undertaken by the Society for Nautical Research. The ship was so intimately wrapped up with the drama of Lord Nelson and Lady Hamilton, with the greatest naval victory in British history, and with the thwarting of Bonaparte's projected invasion, that the Navy and the general public rallied to save her.

No. 2 Dock at Portsmouth was made available and alterations (to bring her to her 1805 state) were carried out, using both public subscription and dockyard resources. Of course, a museum ship (no matter how patriotic her message) should not be repaired or maintained by the defence vote, but a polite fiction took care of that. HMS *Victory* was declared the flagship of the local Commander-in-Chief and thus a warship still in commission; and to give substance to this story, HMS *Victory* was, and still is, used a number of times every year for official functions.

Nelson's cot.
Photo: Alexander McKee

Restoration work on the bow in 1987.
Photo: Alexander McKee

The restoration work, begun in 1923, was completed in 1928. Small pieces of surplus timber were sold to help defray costs (I bought a piece when I first went on board in about 1929, at an age when I did not have to duck under the deckbeams). But the decision not to charge for admission (on the grounds that the taxpayer had already paid for the ship) proved to be unwise. The sales of souvenirs, postcards, booklets, etc., on board did not allow HMS *Victory*'s deadliest enemy, the death watch beetle, to be combatted until decay had gone very far.

The present (1988) state of affairs is that possibly some ten to 15 per cent of her original timbers may remain and 35 per cent are claimed to date from the Napoleonic wars. The rest is an extremely skilful replica, some of the blocks for the rigging having been made nearby. The original mass-production machinery of Nelson's time is on display in the Science Museum and Southsea Castle.

During World War II the spars and part of the masts were removed for safety. A 500 lb bomb did land in No. 2 Dock on the night of 10 March 1941, during the Luftwaffe 'blitz' on Portsmouth, but the effect of modern explosives on an ancient vessel was negligible—a hole of no great extent was blown low down in the hull. As she was in a dry dock it failed to sink her.

A *Victory* Museum was opened in 1938, to display associated relics and also the spectacular panorama of Trafalgar by W. L. Wylie. Next door to this building, on one side of the *Victory* arena, is housed the recently donated Nelson-McCarthy Collection. A few hundred yards away is the Royal Naval Museum, successor to the Dockyard Museum of 1906. All are housed in buildings which are themselves old and historic, as are the docks.

However, a visit to HMS *Victory* is no longer free. With the raising of the *Mary Rose* in 1982 and her move from under the seabed at Spithead into No. 3 Dock, 50 feet or so from the stern of HMS *Victory*, followed by the arrival of HMS *Warrior* in 1987, this part of what we now call HM Naval Base instead of Portsmouth Dockyard has been turned into a 'Heritage Area', attracting visitors from all over the world to what is probably the greatest historic ship collection in existence at present. The *Mary Rose* represents the first English battleship to be armed with complete batteries of siege artillery; HMS *Victory* represents virtually the peak of that development and in its most dramatic and popular aspect; while HMS *Warrior*, a giant in comparison, represents the transition stage of the battleship towards modern times—iron construction, armour plating, auxiliary steam propulsion by means of a propeller, but still basically a sailing ship and with an armament in principle little different from that of *Mary Rose*. And all set in the historic part of a modern, working Naval Base, some 70 miles from London.

From the ferry pontoon just outside the Dockyard, boats run frequently to the RN Submarine Museum at Gosport on the opposite side of the harbour, where a modern submarine, together with the Navy's first, are on display and open to visitors.

Address (for details other than group visits)
The Commanding Officer, HMS *Victory*; HM Naval Base, Portsmouth, Hants.
Telephone: (0705) 819604

Opening Times
March to October: 10.00 am to 5.30 Mon to Sat. 1 pm to 5 pm Sun.

November to February: 10.00 am to 4.30 pm Mon to Sat. 1 pm to 4 pm Sun.
Closed Christmas Day. Last tickets sold 40 minutes before closing.

Entrance Fees
October to April £1.50, OAPs and children 5 to 16 90p.
May to September £1.80, OAPs and children 5 to 16 £1.00.
School and college group rates: 50p all year.

Mary Rose: King Henry VIII's Great Ship

HISTORY

Built at Portsmouth for Henry VIII	1509-10
Took on her guns at the Tower	1511
Crippled the French flagship at Battle of Brest	1512
First sea trials	1513
Rebuilt and rearmed	1536
Sunk by accident in Battle off Portsmouth	1545
Wreck discovered by fishermen and early divers	1836
Wreck deliberately rediscovered by Alexander McKee	1966
Wreck recovered by Mary Rose Trust	1982

SPECIFICATIONS
Probable dimensions based on measurements made after the recovery of the hull (which is one-sided and lacks both stem and forecastle:

Length of keel	32m (105 ft) measured
Length at waterline	37.3m (122 ft 3 ins) estimated
Breadth	11.4m (37 ft 6 ins) estimated
Draught	4.5m (14 ft 9 ins) estimated
Maximum preserved height of hull (fore end of stern castle on starboard side)	13.00m (42 ft 7½ ins)

ARMAMENT
Inventories before and after 1536 rebuild:

1514: 600 tons, 400 men   1545: 700 tons, 415 men
Brass Guns (7 heavy, 6 light)   *Brass Guns* (14 heavy, 1 light)

The *Mary Rose* in the ship hall in 1986, after the hull had been raised upright.
Photo: Mary Rose Trust

Great Curtalls	5	Cannons	2
Murderers	2	Demi-Cannons	2
Falcons	2	Culverins	2
Falconettes	3	Demi-Culverins	6
Little Gun (chambered)	1	Sakers	2
		Falcons	1
Iron Guns (34 heavy, 31 light)		*Iron Guns* (24 heavy, 52 light)	
Great Murderers	1	Port Pieces	12
Murderers	1	Slings	2
Cast Pieces	2	Demi-Slings	3
Murderers	1	Quarter-Slings	1
Slings	3	Fowlers	6
Stone Guns	26	Bases	30
Top Guns	3	Top Pieces	2
Serpentines	28	Hailshot Pieces	20
	Total 78		Total 91
+ Hagboches	91?	+ Handguns	50

When Henry VIII came to the throne as a teenager in 1509, the land and sea forces he inherited were outdated. Continental warfare had been revolutionised by improved siege artillery and the weapons systems created to employ it to greatest effect. Castles and fortified towns, which had hitherto resisted long sieges, were now falling to an attacker in weeks, even days. It was only a matter of time before the same system was employed in ships—but they would have to be vessels specially built to mount complete batteries of siege artillery, flanked by bowmen and pikemen.

In the first year of his reign Henry ordered the building at Portsmouth of two ships to the new continental design, to be armed largely with continental siege weapons emplaced behind gunports. At the same time, he discouraged the use of crossbows and handguns in favour of the retention of the longbow which, provided that trained, practised bowmen existed in sufficient numbers, would be a deadly effective weapon for the second stage of battle, after the guns had shaken and dismayed the enemy. And he retained the pikemen for the final assault.

So Portsmouth Dockyard was then a busy place. One of the big battleships he had inherited, the four-masted *Sovereign*, was being rebuilt in one dock, while the two brand new ships, *Mary Rose* and *Peter Pomegranate*, were building in another. The first was to be his new fleet flagship and was named after his favourite sister; the latter was named for his wife, Katherine of Aragon.

The principal difference between the new ships and the old was that while the main armament of the previous century's warships had been a battalion of infantry backed up by many light guns, the new ships packed a main punch of big guns of various types, backed up by smaller weapons and an infantry complement reduced to two companies of bowmen and pikemen. In 1512, the crew of the *Mary Rose* were listed as 220 soldiers, 20 gunners, 120 mariners, 5 trumpeters, 20 servants, and 26 members of the Admiral's staff. By 1545, her complement of soldiers had been reduced to 185, the gunners increased to 30, the mariners increased to 200—and the ship uprated after her rebuild to 700 instead of 600 tons. These were Tudor tons of course, probably related to a merchantman's cargo-carrying capacity, rather than the displacement tonnage used by modern navies (or the many different types of tonnage measurement lately used by modern merchant vessels).

The whole point about my search for the *Mary Rose*, which began in 1962, was that virtually everything about her—and any ship like her or contemporary with her—was unknown. As far as nautical historians were concerned, she might just as well have been a Martian Flying Saucer. Consider just the gun lists quoted (with modernised spelling) from the original documents I studied more than 20 years ago: the cannons, culverins and falcons were known types, but the rest were names only—what those names represented

Personal items found in the wreck (above), shown with a decorative pouch, and (*below*) a delicate carving of angels in bone, found in a chest on the main deck. They may have formed part of the spine of a book. *Photos: Mary Rose Trust*

in terms of Tudor hardware was unknown. Now, at least there is actual Tudor weaponry to argue about.

And there is a good deal more. Casualty figures vary (as ever); we know that very few escaped, probably no more than three dozen, because the bulk of her crew were below decks or had boarding netting above them; but the number of men aboard varies with the source, from a 'low' of 400 to a 'high' of 700. It is possible that extra infantry were drafted on board for a battle so close to shore, but 700 is probably too high. However, I estimated that some 200 bodies might remain in and around the wreck, and this proved to be correct.

We can now say, which we could not do from documents, that most were in their late teens or early twenties (younger than the *Victory's* crew but pretty much the average for a war, ancient or modern), with a few boys and some men in their forties; average height was 5 ft 7½ ins (killing stone dead the popular idea that our ancestors were undersized); all were healthy but there was evidence of deficiencies in diet during childhood. Their clothing, equipment and personal possessions—some very smart and sophisticated—bring them very close to us as individuals; but, alas, we do not know the name of a single one of them.

Taken together, they represent a fair selection of Tudor naval and military society, ranging across the classes from the aristocracy downwards; suddenly extinguished in the space of a few seconds as

The *Mary Rose* sinking, from a drawing by dell'Orco. *Photo: Alexander McKee*

the ship heeled over to starboard, the water rushed in through the open gunports (for the *Mary Rose* was going into action against a French invasion fleet at Spithead) and the ship sank, taking down with her virtually everyone except a fortunate few who were not trapped. A Flemish survivor told the Imperial ambassador that there had been 500 men aboard, all being drowned 'save about 25 or 30 servants, sailors and the like', and that 'when she heeled over with the wind the water entered by the lowest row of gunports which had been left open after firing'. It was a standard risk with all such ships right into the nineteenth century, just as modern car ferries have their own inbuilt vulnerability.

The English accounts stress bad shiphandling as a contributory factor, together with indiscipline; and a ship expert has made the surely valid point that as ships get older (the *Mary Rose* had been rebuilt 10 years before), so they tend to accumulate a mass of clutter above the waterline—all extra weight in the wrong place. The French, quite naturally, because they had been firing at her shortly before, claimed that it was their guns which sank her; but the recovered hull shows no evidence of this. They were not the first, and they will not be the last, to claim an optimistic 'kill'.

The French fleet of 235 ships was unable to budge the English fleet of about 60 ships out of their defensive position in the tricky shallows of Spitsand; they landed some thousands of men in the Isle of Wight, hoping to tempt Henry out to give battle at sea while heavily out-numbered, but found that he was reinforcing his army garrison in the Wight so effectively that their four beach-heads became untenable; eventually they went home without achieving anything. The mast, yards and sails of the *Mary Rose*, together with some guns, were recovered between 1545 and 1549, but Tudor attempts to raise the sunken hull failed (because there was a very soft seabed at that point and she had sunk in deeply and immediately begun to fill with sediments). Parts of the wreck were visible at low water during Elizabethan times and the site must have made good fishing for at least a century (the first coin we recovered was dated 1610).

Gradually, the lighter portions of the upperworks collapsed, while the heavier timbers of the main hull, exposed above the seabed, became soft and were eaten by marine organisms, mainly gribble but also some teredo. Oyster spat had settled, and when they died their shells littered the site. Finally, virtually nothing was left showing above the seabed bar the eroded tops of a few ribs and just part of a large bronze gun.

This was the scene that met John Deane's eyes in 1836 when, while

Watercolour from John Deane's portfolio of the three bronze guns he raised from the *Mary Rose* in 1836. Top: 68 pdr cannon royal; centre: 9-pdr culverin bastard; bottom: 32-pdr demi-cannon. *Photo: Alexander McKee*

working to salvage the bronze guns of the 1st Rate *Royal George* (sunk in 1782, in deeper water), he was called away by Gosport fishermen who had snagged their gear on an obstruction half-a-mile distant. Of course, they all guessed it was a wreck. John and his brother Charles had invented a simple and effective form of diving gear, which had one drawback: the diver had to keep more or less upright or the helmet would flood freely from below; so John used a rope ladder to descend the 40-50 feet or so to this 'fastener' and was astounded by what he saw. There was no upstanding wreck here at all, merely the remains of a ship so old, and sunk so long ago, that it 'was so completely buried in the sand that the diver could find nothing to which he could affix a rope'. But resting on it, protruding slightly, were two bronze guns with the Tudor Rose plain to see and two wrought-iron breech-loaders of a pattern that some nineteenth century experts had never realised existed. One of the bronze guns was a cannon royal, heavier than anything carried by the giant three-decker *Royal George*.

Because the guns might still belong to the Crown, the Board of Ordnance set up a committee which reported that the wreck must certainly be that of the *Mary Rose*, and encouraged Deane to continue with work which was now more than mere salvage for scrap metal. Deane's last season on the site was 1840, after which he sold many relics at a Portsmouth auction. Subsequently, the site was forgotten again. To try to find it, from 1962 onwards, I searched in many fields. One was to research the pioneer divers, which led me to discover some watercolour paintings made by Deane of some of his recoveries from the *Mary Rose* and a dozen other wrecks. Another route connected with Deane was the discovery of an Admiralty chart of 1841, showing the true site of the *Mary Rose* (the histories gave four different areas, all of them wrong).

John Deane had first seen the *Mary Rose* site on 16 June, 1836, when only a few faint traces on the seabed indicated what might lie beneath. I first dived the *Mary Rose* site on 14 May, 1966, 130 years afterwards. I expected the wreck to be completely invisible now; and it was. I could see for about five feet across a depressing grey plain of clay and mud, with some patches of sand and layer-lines of slipper limpet shells; even if a few frame-tops had been showing for half-an-inch or so, as in Deane's day, the shifting waves of limpets could conceal them. My companion thrust his arm down into the seabed—and it vanished up to the shoulder. A heavy ship would sink deeply here and be well preserved, but just where on that plain was the burial place of the carrack, and even if we knew, how could we

The *Mary Rose* in dock, in February 1983. *Photo: Alexander McKee*

Small bronze watch bell found in the wreck. The inscription reads: 'I was made in the year 1510' (the year the *Mary Rose* was completed). *Photo: Mary Rose Trust*

get down to it? Just how we managed it is described in two books I wrote, the first in 1973, the second in 1982.*

None of the ships described in this book was saved without great effort and, in almost every case, saved against opposition of various sorts. One form we encountered concerned the bodies of the drowned seamen and troops, 'wrenched' from the seabed, as some sentimental protesters aver; while others accuse us of having 'pillaged' a 'grave'. The point about the men of the *Mary Rose* is that, far from being forgotten, as was the case when I began my seabed search in 1965, they are being studied and their personal possessions, on view in the *Mary Rose* exhibition, just inside the dockyard gates, make them as individuals very real to modern people. They have achieved a kind of immortality which would not have been theirs had the *Mary Rose* recovered from her heel and carried on into battle on that July day in 1545.

When you visit the Naval Base, the *Mary Rose* Exhibition is about 50 yards to your right as you enter, the HMS *Warrior* box office directly opposite to your left. The two wooden ship hulls lie about 200 yards straight ahead, passing the Royal Naval Museum on the way to the *Victory* arena. Many visitors find the *Mary Rose* exhibition by far the most interesting, so vivid a picture of life aboard a Tudor warship does it give; there is an introductory film showing at regular intervals. Some people prefer to see the film first, followed by the Exhibition, and then visit the *Mary Rose* ship hall to see the hull; and from there it is a step to HMS *Victory*. Others prefer to visit the ship hall first.

* *King Henry VIII's Mary Rose* (Souvenir Press, 1973) and *How We Found the Mary Rose* (Souvenir Press, 1982).

THE MARY ROSE

The empty hull of the *Mary Rose*, from an artist's impression. *Reproduced by kind permission of Shell UK.*

The hull was totally excavated on the seabed, and therefore it is empty at present; in addition, many of the deck half-beams, deck planking, and partitions were removed to make excavation easier and safer. As conservation proceeds, these are being put back in their original positions. The chill and mist in the ship hall, and also the 'locks' through which one enters to view the hull, are a necessary part of the conservation process and are designed to prevent the timber from drying out, shrinking and distorting. Without the benefit of a human figure (or a realistic dummy), the hull seems smaller than it really is; also, because the contents have been removed, there is little to indicate what each deck was actually used for. These are matters which could be remedied when conservation is complete in perhaps 15 to 20 years from now.

Address (for details other than group visits)
Public Relations Office, Mary Rose Trust, College Road, HM Naval Base, Portsmouth, PO1 3LX.
Telephone: (0705) 750521

Opening Times
March to October 10.30 am to 5.00 pm every day.
November to February 10.30 am to 5.00 pm every day except Christmas Day.
Last tickets sold one hour before closing.

Entrance Fees
October to April £2.50, OAPs and children 5 to 16 £1.50.
May to September £2.80, OAPs and children 5 to 16 £1.80.
School and college group rates: October to April £1.00, May to September £1.25.

HMS *Warrior*: 'The Black Snake'

HISTORY
Built at Thames Ironworks, Blackwall   1859-60
Sea trials   1861
First commission   1862

No longer classed as a 1st Rate   1871
Withdrawn from sea service   1883
Became depot ship *Vernon III*   1904
Who'll buy my old frigate?   1924
Became Oil Fuel Hulk C77, Pembroke Dock   1929
Handed to Maritime Trust for restoration, Hartlepool   1979
Towed to Portsmouth to join *Victory* and *Mary Rose*   1987

SPECIFICATIONS

Length overall	127.4m (418 ft)
Length between perpendiculars	115.8m (380 ft)
Beam	17.7m (58 ft)
Mean draught	7.9m (26 ft)
Displacement	9,210 tons
Complement	700

ORIGINAL ARMAMENT

26 68-pdr (8.2 in) smooth-bore muzzle-loaders
10 110-pdr (7 in) Armstrong rifled-bore breech-loaders
4 40-pdr (4.7 in) Armstrong rifled-bore breech-loaders
Armament concentrated in a central citadel 213 ft long, 22 ft deep, protected by $4\frac{1}{2}$-inch wrought-iron plates backed by 18 inches of teak.

STEAM PROPULSION

Penn's horizontal trunk type two cylinder engines, double acting, jet condensing. Cylinders 112 in diameter by 4 ft stroke. Nominal 1,250 hp. Boilers: 10 rectangular fire tubes with 40 furnaces and a steam pressure of 22 psi. Coal bunkers for 850 tons. Rate of consumption: $12\frac{1}{2}$ tons an hour = 68 hours steaming = 1,000 miles. Two-bladed 24 ft diameter Griffiths lifting-type propeller. Two 31 ft telescopic funnels.

SAIL PROPULSION

Square-rigged on three masts to scale of an 80-gun ship of the line with 48,400 sq ft of canvas.

Speed under sail	13 knots
Maximum recorded speed under steam	14 knots
Maximum recorded speed under sail and steam	$17\frac{1}{2}$ knots

Crew: 50 officers, 75 stokers, 125 marines (i.e., soldiers), 380 seamen.

The result of the Napoleonic wars, and in particular the crushing British victory at Trafalgar, was to give Britain virtually worldwide domination of the seas, protection for her trade, and security against

HMS *Warrior* at anchor, seen from the multi-storey car park nearby. *Photo: Alexander McKee*

invasion from any military power, no matter how numerous or efficient its army. All this was put at risk when, in March 1858, the French ordered six ships of a revolutionary new type to be built, the first being *La Gloire*.

No significant changes had taken place since Trafalgar: the battleship was still a high-sided wooden wall, slightly larger and near to the limit for building in wood. But a range of new technologies had become available, notably steam power and iron construction, which had been pioneered at sea by the builders of merchant ships. Brunel's SS *Great Britain* of 1843 (see p. 66) and his gigantic *Great Eastern* of 1858, which was 680 feet long, had overcome the objections of those theorists who declared that iron does not float. Having invested in wooden sailing ships, the Navy was reluctant to undertake experiments which, if successful, must make them all obsolete. Also, iron hulls were not impervious to solid shot hurled from smooth-bore muzzle-loaders, and to use flimsy paddles in war was to invite speedy disaster to the propulsion mechanism, which in any event was still far from efficient.

A new chief designer and constructor for the French Navy, Dupuy de Lôme, forced a rethink upon his British opponents. He ordered that no more ships be constructed of wood: all were to be of iron. But

Warrior's retractable funnel, designed to reduce wind-resistance when she was under sail. *Photo: Alexander McKee*

because the Industrial Revolution was less far advanced in France, the first three of the new programme had to be built with wooden hulls faced with wrought-iron armour plate. *La Gloire*, the first of them, was completed in August 1860. She was still a sailing ship, but with an auxiliary steam engine driving a screw, and armour capable of deflecting the heaviest shot from one of Britain's 120-gun wooden walls; with a speed of 13 knots, she could chase the British fleet right out of the Channel, or destroy anything that tried to stand against her. As France had a great army, fully capable of conquering England if only it could be got ashore, the British Admiralty reacted at once.

First thoughts were to copy *La Gloire*—to put iron cladding on wooden ships. The bolder idea, for an iron ship with a great armour-plated citadel amidships, holding most of the armament, eventually won the day. Built of iron, the ship could be much larger than any wooden hull, and could carry far heavier guns; while the *Victory's* heaviest guns were 32-pdrs, *Warrior* could mount mainly 68-pdrs and 110-pdrs. And whereas *La Gloire* was to be 256 ft long, *Warrior's* length was over 400 feet.

No naval dockyard could build *Warrior*; only civilian constructors had the necessary resources to build so large a vessel in iron. She was launched four months after *La Gloire*, and when she joined the Channel Fleet at Portsmouth it was said that, compared to the old wooden walls, 'she looks like a black snake amongst the rabbits'.

Because of her proportions, long and narrow, and her single gun-deck, the die-hards classed her as a frigate—a 5th Rate too weak to lie in the line of battle—but, in fact she was more nearly a clipper in shape (see pp. 41 and 78). In essentials, however, the *Warrior* was still a sailing ship and her armament, in principle, not unlike that of the *Mary Rose*, with its mixture of muzzle-loading and breech-loading guns. The only difference, apart from size, was that the new breech-loaders had rifled barrels and fired cylindrical shells instead of spherical solid shot or hollow 'shell'. A hollow sphere was exploded, not on impact but by a burning time-fuse; while a cylindrical shell had a fuse in the nose—no chance of chucking it overboard while it was fizzing around the deck. But breech-loading still proved unsatisfactory and was not perfected for another 30 years or so.

If you see the three battleships in chronological order, going from *Mary Rose* to *Victory* and then to *Warrior*, one difference is immediately apparent. While in Nelson's ship you have to duck your head under every deck beam, in *Warrior* there is no need to flinch—there is ample height between decks to walk upright. Then,

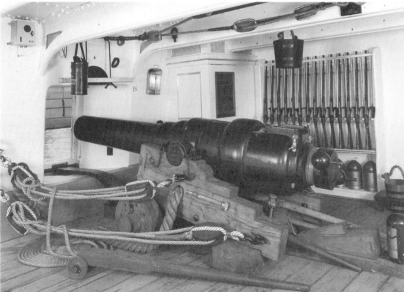

Warrior's great breech-loading guns: (*above*) showing the immense care that has gone into the details of the restoration. *Photo: Alexander McKee*; (*below*) one of the 110-pdr Armstrong guns on the main deck. *Photo: HMS Warrior Trust*

close to the furnaces, and presumably for use mainly by the stokers, there is an actual bathroom with a proper bath and nearby a nineteenth-century laundrette, again presumably largely for the benefit of the stokers, for coal-burning ships involved much filth and dirt.

Warrior represented such a tremendously powerful innovation, backed by superior industrial resources, that French ambitions for glory and revenge at sea faded instantly; truly, *Warrior* and her sister ship *Black Prince* had proved successful deterrents. At the time, they might have appeared the ultimate, bound to rule the waves for as long as the *Victory*, or even *Mary Rose*. But nothing of the sort. Within ten years, they were obsolete.

The trend was towards the opposite of *Mary Rose* and *Victory*; instead of many comparatively small guns, a few really heavy ones; and as the guns increased in size and power, so did the defensive armour. Mechanical systems replaced manpower—*Warrior's* anchors, for instance, had to be raised by hundreds of men working at capstan bars, as in the *Victory*. Steam engines became far more efficient, and the sails could be discarded. Even flogging was abolished in the British Navy. The day of the hybrid ship was gone, but so strongly had the *Warrior* been made that she survived in some form or another, as depot ship or loading pier; and because she was made of wrought-iron, she did not deteriorate as fast as more modern vessels. She survived also because, when occasionally the Admiralty tried to sell her, no one was interested. In this way she became the only surviving nineteenth-century battleship anywhere in the world.

By 1967 serious efforts were being made to save her, and in 1969 the Maritime Trust was formed with the Duke of Edinburgh as founder-President. The successful return of the *Great Britain* from the Falkland Islands in 1970 formed an encouraging precedent for the rescue of really important historic vessels. Part of the finance necessary for restoration was pledged by a former MP, John Smith, through his Manifold Trust. In 1979 the Ministry of Defence announced that the *Warrior* had been handed over to the Maritime Trust, for restoration at Hartlepool on the north-east coast.

Warrior had been reduced to a concrete-covered jetty; her engines and almost all her fittings had been taken out. To recreate her as she was in 1861-64 required immense historical research, as well as detailed scrutiny of the ship as it was cleaned up, to note and record all traces of former fittings. Then replicas had to be constructed of almost everything, from the engines to the guns and their ammunition. Some genuinely contemporary items were obtained, but what strikes one most about the *Warrior* is the immense amount

The main deck steering wheels.   *Photo: HMS Warrior Trust.*

The beautifully restored rigging. *Photo: Alexander McKee*

HMS *Warrior*, Britain's first ironclad, returns to a tumultuous welcome in Portsmouth Harbour on 16 June 1987. *Photo: HMS Warrior Trust*

of work which must have been devoted to thousands of small items, to obtain the intended impression of a battleship which has just tied up at Portsmouth Dockyard and been vacated by the crew only a few minutes ago.

In July 1987 the restored ship was towed in from Hartlepool to a tremendous welcome, the Navy putting on a particularly dramatic display of fireworks and balloons. Now, if one travels to the Naval Base by train, the ship can be seen as one comes out of the station, a few hundred yards away; if one arrives by road, parking in the multi-storey just outside the dockyard, again *Warrior* is visible a few hundred yards distant.

Address (for details other than group visits)
The Visitor Services Manager, HMS *Warrior* 1860, HM Naval Base, Portsmouth, PO1 3LX.
Telephone: (0705) 291379

Opening Times
March to October 10.30 am to 5.30 pm every day.
November to February 10.30 am to 5.00 pm every day except Christmas Day.
Last tickets sold one hour before closing.

Entrance Fees
All year: £3.00, OAPs £2.50, children 5 to 16 £1.50.

---

2 THE GOSPORT SIDE

Gosport is on the west side of Portsmouth Harbour, the operational Submarine Base—a 'stone frigate' named HMS *Dolphin*—and the associated RN Submarine Museum being by the harbour entrance which had a gun fort erected at an early date and is still referred to by the descriptive title of 'Blockhouse'. One end of the 'Great Chain' which could be raised to block the entrance to the port was secured here, the other being by Round Tower on the Portsmouth shore.

To the north of Gosport is Priddy's Hard which has an armaments museum, sometimes open to visitors by arrangement.

Until 1987, two wooden warships were moored off the Gosport side, the sloop *Gannet* which has irrevocably gone to Chatham Historic Dockyard for renovation and eventual display, and the frigate *Foudroyant* (ex-*Trincomalee*) which is being restored at Hartlepool by the people who dealt with HMS *Warrior* and will probably return to Gosport to continue with her Training Ship role.

HMS *Trincomalee*: The Indian Teak Frigate

HISTORY

Built at Bombay	Mar 1816–Oct 1817
Arrived Portsmouth	1819
Cut down from 46-gun frigate to 26-gun corvette and commissioned at Portsmouth	1847
Commissioned as training ship, RNR	1860
Sold as a boys' training ship and renamed *Foudroyant*	1897

SPECIFICATIONS

Length on lower deck	45.8m (150 ft $4\frac{1}{2}$ ins)
Breadth extreme	12m (39 ft 11 ins)
Depth in hold	4m (12 ft 9 ins)
Burden in tons	1,062 tons
Complement	240

HMS *Trincomalee*, built in Bombay of Indian teak in 1817, and renamed *Foudroyant* in 1912, when she was taken over as a boys' training ship. *Photo: Alexander McKee*

ARMAMENT
As 46-gun frigate:

Upper deck	28 18-pdrs
Quarterdeck	6 9-pdrs
	6 32-pdr carronades
Forecastle	2 9-pdrs
	2 32-pdr carronades

A frigate was a 5th Rate (i.e. not strong enough to lie in the line of battle) and carried most of her armament on one continuous gun-deck. In the first half of the twentieth century her equivalent would have been a cruiser, of which HMS *Belfast* (see p. 85) is an example: powerful enough to crush most opponents, fast enough to escape from stronger ones. Generally, the longer the ship, the faster (except for those which can go up on the plane); built for speed, for scouting and communication and commerce-raiding duties, but lightly constructed, a frigate was more roomy in proportion to her size than a battleship, and could therefore be used also as a troop transport.

This particular frigate was French in conception and Indian in construction, and her building was delayed because the British frigate carrying her plans out to Bombay in 1812 was sunk by a stronger United States frigate. The Navy Office in 1796 had drawn up plans for a frigate called the *Leda*, based on the lines of a captured French frigate, the *Hébé*. For more than 20 years British ships were built to this successful French design, among them two at Portsmouth, *Arethusa* in 1817 and *Minerva* in 1820, together with *Penelope* at Chatham in 1829. Two sister ships to these were to be built at Bombay of Indian teak instead of British oak—*Amphitrite* and *Trincomalee*.

British oak was now in short supply, but that was only part of the

The turbaned Indian which forms the figurehead of the *Trincomalee*. *Photo: Alexander McKee*

reason for having her constructed in India. Teak is a superior wood for this purpose. The unsentimental insurers at Lloyds rated teak as having a useful life in ships of 16 years, English oak at 12, Australian jarra and New Zealand kauri ten years. *Trincomalee* proved their point, as she has survived 170 years afloat. Teak did not splinter easily either in war or peace; seams did not open; its hardness and natural oil repelled the bacteria and other organisms which in course of time consume ship timbers.

At this time the master builder of Bombay Dockyard was Jamsetjee Bomanjee Lowjee, a Parsee of the Wadia family, who had a high reputation both in the Royal Navy and the East India Company. Fittingly, the frigate's figurehead was a turbaned Indian, and instead of being named after Roman and Greek deities she was called *Trincomalee*, after that splendid port in Ceylon. Built in less than 18 months, the formidable frigate was too late for the Napoleonic Wars (Bonaparte having been sent into final exile at St Helena in 1815) and too expensive in manpower to keep in commission in peacetime. So she was laid up in reserve at Portsmouth until 1845—nearly 30 years.

The frigate was then converted to a 26-gun corvette; fewer guns but heavier ones, and fewer men to man them. The conversion cost £10,000, her building having cost £23,000. She was commissioned in 1847 with a complement of 240—24 officers, 39 Petty Officers, 115 seamen, 33 boys, 29 Royal Marines. They were short-service volunteers, but soon the peacetime Navy would need a proper career structure. Rations were improving—tea as well as rum and lime-juice, meat often in tins instead of casks and water in fitted metal tanks.

Trincomalee sailed for the West Indies and patrolled the Caribbean, which was in turmoil; the United States was having a war with Mexico and the former Spanish possessions were in a state of constant disturbance, while illegal slave traders were bringing in human cargoes in very fast vessels.

Her next commission, which began in 1852, was in the Pacific, where again there was a flourishing slave trade run by the 'blackbirders'. While there, war broke out between Britain and France on the one side and Russia on the other—which made something of a change; but the Russians had only six vessels in the Pacific to challenge the Allied fleet of 26, and wisely would not engage. The armament of the *Trincomalee* at this time consisted of 14 43-pounders firing solid shot, ten 8-inch shell guns and one 10-inch shell gun on a revolving mounting (the latter causing stability problems). They were never fired in anger.

The deck of the *Trincomalee* during her training ship days, crowded with boats for the use of cadets. *Photo: Alexander McKee*

By the time of the *La Gloire-Warrior* confrontation, the *Trincomalee* was obsolete and in 1860 she became a training ship for the new Royal Naval Reserve at South Shields, then at Hartlepool, finally at Southampton. In 1897 she was put up for sale at £1,323.

She was saved from being made into furniture by the wreck the same year of a much more historic vessel, HMS *Foudroyant* of 80 guns, copied in 1789 from a French prize, which had been Nelson's flagship in the Mediterranean in 1799-1800. In 1891 *Foudroyant* was sold for breaking up to a German firm, but was purchased by Mr G.W. Cobb of Chepstow, whose idea was to restore her as a working historic ship, which would tour coastal resorts and also be used for training boys to the sea. He paid £6,000 for her, spent a further £20,000 on her restoration, and was on a training tour and off Blackpool when a gale drove her aground. Cobb and the six-man crew and the boy trainees sang various appropriate hymns—'Hearts of Oak', 'Eternal Father, strong to save'—until the gale died down and they could be rescued. But the ship herself was beyond saving and was duly turned into certificated '*Foudroyant* furniture', ranging from a replica of 'a chair belonging to Lord Nelson's father' to ping pong racquets at 1/9d, egg timers at 1/–, and collar studs at 1d each.

But Wheatley Cobb would not give up: he bought the *Trincomalee*, renamed her *Foudroyant*, and continued with his boys' training scheme, a role which the ship was carrying out until 1987, ninety years later. Of course the Bombay frigate did not have the historical associations of the battleship, whose deck had seen Lady Hamilton pleading for the life of Prince Caraccioli, been temporarily the site of the court of the kingdom of Naples, had beaten the French 80-gun *Guillaume Tell* into surrender in two hours and 20 minutes during the blockade of Malta in 1800, and had earlier taken part in the capture of the *Hoche* and her consorts, part of a French fleet aiding a rebellion in Ireland in 1798.

The next crisis for the *Trincomalee/Foudroyant* was just after the Second World War, which had exhausted and impoverished Britain. At that time there were a number of genuinely historic vessels still afloat (for which any seaside city would now give all its ratepayers' eye-teeth). At the back of Portsmouth Harbour, for instance, was HMS *Implacable*, 80 guns, built at Toulon in 1797 as the *Duguay-Trouin,** which in 1805 had fought at Trafalgar on the other side and escaping from that disaster, was brought to action by Sir Richard Strachan and, although still crippled, 'fought to admiration', suffering 150 men killed (including her captain, Claude Touffet), before hauling down her flag. Under British colours, she served in the Baltic and in 1808 fought yard-arm to yard-arm with the Russian 74-gun *Sevelod* and took her. She, too, was eventually acquired by Mr Wheatley Cobb through the intervention of King Edward VII, who was dismayed by the Admiralty's decision in 1908 to scrap her. She was towed to Falmouth where she served as a boys' training ship, and when Mr Cobb's resources proved inadequate to cover the next refit, the 'Implacable' Committee of the Society for Nautical Research stepped in and raised sufficient funds by public subscription. Then came the Second World War in 1939-45, and a need was perceived by the Admiralty for both *Trincomalee* and *Duguay-Trouin* to serve the war effort against Hitler as floating storeships in Portsmouth Harbour. The old French muskets were still in the hold of *Duguay-Trouin* when, in 1940, the Stukas came screaming down on Portsmouth Harbour, and a French battleship lately escaped from the fall of France, the *Courbet*, anchored nearby, her sides winking with the yellow flashes of gunfire, shot the tail off a Junkers 88.

* René Duguay-Trouin (1673–1737), privateer.

"CENTAUR" AND "IMPLACABLE" CAPTURE THE "SEVOLOD," 26TH AUGUST, 1808.

HMS *Implacable* engaging with the Russian warship *Sevelod* in the Baltic in 1808.
Photo: Ilse McKee (McKee Collection)

The business of the Admiralty is not to preserve old ships but to build and operate new ones, so one should not be too harsh on what now appears short-sightedness; but in December, 1946 there was much critical comment in the letters columns of *The Times.*

Sir, I note that two of our few remaining ships from 'Nelson's stirring times' are very likely to be broken up. Can no authority or body be brought to interest themselves in the matter by providing a resting place for them similar to that given to the *Victory*? It is not credible that their timbers are not also able to bear their ships' weight in dry dock, and many would gladly subscribe to their preservation.—John Randles.

Sir, I am sure many readers will endorse Mr John Randles' remarks concerning the threat to those grand old ships *Implacable* and *Foudroyant*. The former was restored before the war at a cost of £20,000, which was subscribed by the public following a nation-wide appeal. Although one fully appreciates the practical difficulties involved in caring for these very old ships, it is absurd to suggest, as your original report seems to do, that six years of war-time neglect could have caused such extensive deterioration following the expensive restoration of a few years before. The Admiralty, in fact, seem to be incapable of looking properly after any historic ships entrusted to their care. The *Victory* herself was allowed to rot to pieces at her moorings, and was only saved at the last minute at the eleventh hour—again by public subscription.—G.F.B. Robinson.

Sir, I should like to endorse what Mr Robinson says about the Admiralty's seeming incapability of looking after historic ships, and for that reason I look upon it as useless to try to preserve the *Implacable* and *Foudroyant*. I often pass by the old *Victory*, and it breaks my heart to see her as she now is, with her masts badly stayed and rigging all anyhow.—Captain, R.N. (Retired).

A final plea in 1947 quoted from Dr A. Conan Doyle, creator of Sherlock Holmes but also of a poem lamenting the sale of the real *Foudroyant* (Nelson's) to a German ship-breakers back in 1897:

> Who says the Nation's purse is lean,
>   Who fears for claim or bond or debt,
> When all the glories that have been
>   Are scheduled as a cash asset?
> If times are bad and trade is slack,
>   If coal and cotton fail at last,
> We've something left to barter yet – – –
>   Our glorious past.

The old *Duguay-Trouin/Implacable* was sentenced to die on 2 December 1949. She could simply have been left to decay a little further until financial times changed; but no. She could have been given back to the French to preserve; but no. She could even have been broken up and the wood sold for souvenirs; but no. At least the muskets did not go down with her; a man I know removed them all to the *Trincomalee/Foudroyant*, before 'the old Implacable', as the press called her, went out of Portsmouth under tow for the last time. For the ship had been condemned to be publicly sunk.

The Navy do these things very well, with a good deal of ceremony, the French flag as well as the British flying on the doomed hulk, warships in attendance, everyone invited (even the French and the Society for Nautical Research), half the world's press (it was said) and many newsreel cameramen. The Commander-in-Chief was present.

At 1.45 pm, ten miles SE of the Owers light vessel, in 36 fathoms, the four scuttling charges were blown. A cloud of black smoke and debris spurted upwards, and the *Duguay-Trouin/*HMS *Implacable* settled quickly in the water. And then stopped. The colours had been half-masted, the ship's companies fallen in, the buglers had sounded the Last Post—but the upper deck of the Trafalgar veteran remained above the waves, flags defiantly flying. When the last spectator vessel left the scene, what the Navy claimed was that only the upper deck of *Implacable* was still afloat, an ominous black line in the water. The tug *Alligator*, with a wreck buoy slung over her bow, ready to mark the spot, was left looking rather foolish. The last act, late in the day, was the crashing and thumping of the two tugs, *Alligator* and *Excluder*, repeatedly ramming the wreck to encourage it to sink and/or disintegrate. This was later to be described as an effort to beach her.

The *Trincomalee/Foudroyant* was saved, but only with difficulty. She made several journeys to Southampton to be repaired, during one of which a witness observed that 'she slipped through the water like a racing yacht'. Her most recent departure, in July 1987, was quite different, and attracted a considerable media audience. Of course, the whole scene had changed since the raising of the *Mary Rose*, which had served to accelerate the slow process of turning part of Portsmouth Dockyard into a possible heritage area, as the dockyard itself was run down.

The move of the *Foudroyant* (ex-*Trincomalee*) was an enormous contrast to the pessimistic despatch of *Implacable* in 1949. No tugs now, but a submersible barge, *Goliath Pacific* of Rotterdam, 450 ft long, 102 ft wide, able to lift 1,700 tons. When we arrived, only the far ends of *Goliath* were visible; occupying only a small part of the watery space between them was the *Foudroyant*, perched high up in the air, some of her timbers in a very bad way indeed. Coyly queuing up to go on next was the *Minerva*, a 540-ton Monitor built at Belfast by Harland & Wolff under the Emergency War Programme of 1915; her dimensions were $170 \times 31 \times 6\frac{1}{2}$ feet, the shallow draught comparing to *Foudroyant*'s 19 feet. She was built for coastal bombardment duties and might have to go into shallow water; her bombardment gear consisted (in her heyday) of two 6-inch guns, and her speed of 10 knots made her slower than either *Warrior* or *Foudroyant*. But she had seen war service in the Mediterranean, Aegean Sea and White Sea; and now, in 1987, was considered worthy of restoration also (although her final port of display is undecided). *Foudroyant* will probably come back again to the Gosport side of Portsmouth Harbour, where she was moored for many years, in her old role of boys' training ship—unless there is

(*Above*) The *Trincomalee* on board the pontoon *Goliath Pacific* in July 1987, before setting out on her journey to Hartlepool. (*Below*) the *Minerva* waits to join the *Trincomalee* on the pontoon. *Photos: Alexander McKee*

lurking in the wings someone whose offers cannot be refused. In this way, Gosport lost HMS *Gannet*, again in 1987.

The sight of *Goliath Pacific* sailing off into the dawn with no less than two historic ships on board, both bound for restoration at Hartlepool, made one realise that what we had unwittingly helped to start with a 15-ft boat and a handful of divers back in 1965, had become big business indeed.

Royal Navy Submarine Museum, Gosport: 'A Damned un-English Weapon'

The museum is part of the submarine base, a 'stone frigate' called HMS *Dolphin* after a real wooden frigate once moored there as a depot. It is also a memorial to the 5,073 submariners who have lost their lives in war and also, alas, in peacetime, and is probably the finest museum of its kind in the world, telling the story of submersible craft from Elizabethan days to the monstrous nuclear vessels which are the 'capital' ships of modern navies.

Holland I, the oldest submarine on display at the Royal Navy Submarine Museum.
Photo: Alexander McKee

There is a model of the *Turtle*, the world's first operational attack submarine which worked well enough in 1776 to attempt an abortive mission against the flagship of the British fleet then blockading New York; considering that the craft had to be pedalled by the one-man crew, it was a brave effort.

The oldest genuine article on display (which may be entered) also has an American lineage. It is called Holland I after its inventor, John Phillip Holland, an Irish monk, fanatically anti-British, who emigrated to America and, funded by the Irish-American community, set about designing a submersible to sink the fleet of Ireland's ancient enemy. By 1900 his Holland VI proved good enough to receive orders from, not only the US Navy, but the British Royal Navy as well. The Admiralty ordered five of the class to be built under licence by Vickers at Barrow-in-Furness; and the first was completed in 1905. This is the 'boat' now generally known as Holland I, which foundered without loss of life while in tow to the breaker's yard in 1913; was deliberately discovered off Plymouth at the request of the museum in 1981; raised in 1982; partially restored and is now on display.

She is tiny, only 63 feet long—and the reason why submarines were first called 'boats' (a 'ship' then being defined as a vessel which is big enough to carry boats). The tradition has remained unaltered, although a modern submarine may be over 400 feet long and displace many thousands of tons.* Holland I displaced 122 tons when dived and was supposed to be able to go to 100 feet (but fortunately never did); she had a crew of eight; her main engine was a four-cylinder petrol engine made in America in the 1890s, which could drive the boat at 7.4 knots on the surface; submerged, on the electric motor, she could do three hours at 6-7 knots. She was armed with one torpedo tube. What you see inside is a little bare, because she had been stripped of all useful gear before being sent to the breakers, and her interior is in process of restoration. In war, a former commander said, she would have been almost totally useless, and could easily swamp in any sort of sea because of the tiny conning tower; but her hull foreshadowed the shapes of the nuclear 'boats' still to come.

The British Admiralty was firmly anti-submarine—and with reason. As far back as 1804, even before Trafalgar, Earl St Vincent had said: 'Pitt is the greatest fool that ever existed to encourage a mode of warfare which those who command the seas do not want and, if successful, will deprive them of it.' The Admiralty had

---

* In the days of sail, the definition referred to the rig, not the hull.

ordered submarines merely in order to evaluate them. Rightly, they feared them because the invention of the self-propelled Whitehead torpedo gave previously laughable 'boats' a deadly sting, striking a ship underwater. In 1900 they had scoffed at them as 'weapons of the weaker power', but the Controller of the Navy gave the game away by saying, 'Submariners should be hanged as pirates in wartime.' The fearful fury was justified. World War I at sea opened with the sinking, by one small German submarine, of three British cruisers one after the other inside an hour. In both World Wars Britain came very close to defeat by the U-boat. Her enemies were far less dependent on seaborne supplies than she was; although RN submarines played a large part in the defeat of the Axis forces in North Africa by cutting off much of their supplies.

Also on display are even smaller midget submarines from the Second World War—an Italian human torpedo, a German *Biber* and a British X-Craft.

The main 'boat' on display, however, is HMS *Alliance* which was designed for service against the Japanese in the Pacific, where the vast distances put range, surface speed, spare torpedo capacity and

A midget submarine from the Second World War—the British X-Craft. *Photo: Alexander McKee*

HMS *Alliance*, the standard type of pre-nuclear submarine. *Photo: Ilse McKee*

even a little comfort for the crew as necessary requirements. She was completed in 1947, too late for the war, but looking just like any other submarine of her time until, in 1958-60, she was refitted, streamlined and modernised. Her displacement now was 1,385 tons on the surface, 1,620 tons submerged; complement five officers and 63 ratings. Her torpedo tubes were reduced to four in the bow and two in the stern with ten reload torpedoes. Streamlining produced a better top submerged speed, 10 knots as compared to 8, increased her range and above all, made her quieter. Maximum surface speed was about 18 knots; fully submerged at $2\frac{1}{2}$ knots she could stay down for up to 36 hours. (The nuclear 'boats', which are the first true submarines, not just surface vessels which can go underwater for a short time, can stay down for an almost unlimited time).

HMS *Alliance* is now supported on concrete blocks, wholly in air, so that the hull lines, ballast tanks, diving planes and so on can be appreciated. Holes have been cut in the hull fore and aft so that visitors can enter near the bow, at the forward torpedo stowage compartment, then walk right down the vessel to the aft torpedo compartment. The Mark VIII torpedoes, usually fired in a spread, would run to 5,000 yards at 45 knots, but the ideal range was 1,200 yards, which left the target less time to dodge.

The huge conning tower of the *Alliance* (*left*) compared with the tiny one on Holland I. *Photos: Alexander McKee*

The stowage compartment also contained one of the circular escape hatches. Naturally, the hatch would not open until the compartment had been flooded and the air in it compressed so that it equalled the pressure of the water outside—which might be only 100 feet but perhaps very much more. Meanwhile, as the water rose around them, the men would breath pure air from a built-in system. A twill trunk would be pulled down from the hatch, and when it was time to go to the surface, each man would duck under the twill trunking and find nothing between himself and the surface but 100 feet of water—or whatever the depth might be. At one time the use of Davis Escape Apparatus was all the rage, but as these sets contained pure oxygen, which can become poisonous in as little as 30 feet of water, it was gradually realised that the safety apparatus was actually convulsing people; it would be safer to let them go up with no breathing apparatus at all, and this is what is now taught at the Submarine Escape Tower at HMS *Dolphin* (a noted local landmark). It seems to work quite well even at 300 feet (when both the nitrogen and the oxygen in breathing air becomes poisonous), and there have been experimental test escapes from as deep as 600 feet (but with some 'bends' casualties). However, the men are now equipped with protective suits, because there have been instances of survivors reaching the surface alive from a sunken submarine and, because there was no one to pick them up, dying of cold and exposure within a very short time.

Walking aft through accommodation spaces shows how extremely cramped is life in a conventional submarine; there are not enough bunks for everyone, so men coming off watch would have to get into a 'hot' bunk just vacated by someone else. And as water was at a premium, very little washing could be done; everyone smelled; and in war, no one got very much sleep because the klaxon was likely to bring everyone to diving stations instantly, and of course they all had to sleep in their clothes.

While the tiny size of the kitchen, designed to produce meals for 60 men, will amaze housewives, it is the search periscope in the control room which makes a hit with their children. It has a round-about seat which turns on the press of a footpedal and is great fun with both girls and boys; a twist grip allows the operator with one hand to search vertically for aircraft, while with the other hand he can alter the magnification. For keeping continuous watch while running just submerged and using the 'snort' tube to bring air into the boat, this is a convenient way of controlling a heavy instrument. The attack periscope is smaller and lighter, being used to pop up for a brief few seconds' look in the final stages of an attack, hopefully without attracting attention. Both the periscopes incorporate a range-finder.

The submarine was controlled by three men—a helmsman for the rudder and two hydroplane operators—one for the fore-planes controlling the depth, the other for the after-planes which regulated the bow-up or bow-down attitude of the boat. If completely neutral buoyancy could be achieved, the boat could hover in mid-water.

Although, in order to submerge, air from the tanks she was riding on had to be released and water let in, the process had to be reversed at depth—for every 100 feet she went down, the submarine had to be made lighter by pumping out 45 gallons. The reason (which every diver who wears a wet-suit will appreciate), is that the hull (like the suit) shrinks with increasing pressure, becomes smaller, and so displaces less water. 'Compressibility was quite noticeable when going deep: the radar office wooden door, for instance, had a habit of bending as the enormous pressure of water squeezed the submarine'. So the boat had to be made lighter by pumping out water, or she would carry on sinking until the hull collapsed. Normal maximum depth for *Alliance* was 500 feet, but there was a considerable safety factor.

The author dwarfed by the massive stern of HMS *Alliance. Photo: Ilse McKee*

The trim of the boat altered slightly all the time, partly because of the changing density of the water in different areas, and partly as stores, such as fresh water and oil fuel, were used up and as torpedoes were expended. If there was a sudden, dangerous alteration of trim caused by flooding, the quick answer was to rush sailors in the opposite direction—aft, for instance, if she was down by the bow, as your average sailor weighs the equivalent of 15 gallons.

Like real dolphins and whales, the primary search system of *Alliance* was sonar. Sound travels a long way underwater and the long-range sonar could pick up contacts at around 100 miles, but with poor definition and direction. The large dome on the bow houses the shorter range sonar, which gives a bearing on the target and tells what sort of noise it is making, which helps identification and estimates of its speed. Eventually, all the information coming in to the control room has to be integrated to produce a torpedo firing solution, allowing for the target's speed, course, distance and draught.

In the after end of the control room are the radio and radar offices; both could be used when the submarine was at shallow depth.

A great deal of space is taken up by the main engines—8-cylinder 4-stroke supercharged Vickers diesels rated at 2,150 hp at 450 rpm—and the electric motors with their giant batteries and switchboards for deeper submerged running. Aft of these, in the stern, are two more torpedo tubes plus four reloads and another escape hatch. Noise and vibration, being so near the engines and screws, was the drawback of the accommodation here; distance from the Officers and Chief Petty Officers forward—and a modicum of privacy—was the prized advantage.

Just as the ships in the main heritage area in Portsmouth Dockyard are flanked by modern warships, so this museum gains from being part of an operating submarine base.

How to Get There

By rail from London to Portsmouth Harbour Station (exactly as for *Mary Rose*, *Victory* and *Warrior*), then across the harbour by using the nearby Gosport ferry (which involves a 12-minute walk or No 9 bus ride on the Gosport side), or look for the special ferry boat which goes direct from the station pontoon to HMS *Alliance*. If coming from the west, it might be more convenient to get off the train at Fareham and take a five-mile bus ride.

By road turn off the M27 at Fareham (signed Gosport) and take the A32, following signs for HMS *Dolphin*/Submarine Museum. Ample car parking (small charge for cars).

Address

HMS *Alliance*/RN Submarine Museum, Gosport, Hants, PO12 2AB. Telephone: (0705) 510354, (0705) 529217 (group visit enquiries only)

Opening Times

Every day except 24 December to 2 January:
10.00 am to last tour 4.30 pm (April to October).
10.00 am to last tour 3.30 pm (November to March).

Entrance Fees

Adults £2.00, OAPs and Children £1.20.
Special rates for groups & coaches.

---

3 KENT

HMS *Gannet*: Sloop Strife

HISTORY

Launched at Sheerness	1878
South American cruise ended	1883
Fired on Dervishes, Suakin	1888
Paid off at Sheerness, and became sail training ship	1895
Became HQ RNVR and renamed HMS *President*	1904
Moved to Hamble and renamed *Mercury*	1911
Training school closed down	1968
Taken over by Maritime Trust	1971
Battle for possession and restoration fought by Gosport and Chatham	1987

SPECIFICATIONS

Length	51.8m (170 ft)
Tonnage	1,130
Rigged as a barque with 2-cylinder Humphrey & Tennant horizontal compound engine	1,107 hp
Complement	13 Officers, 27 petty officers, 64 seamen, 11 boys, 24 marines

ARMAMENT
4 carriage-mounted 64-pdr guns
2 7-inch muzzle-loaded rifled guns

HMS *Gannet* was a sloop of the *Osprey* class, designed to carry out patrols over great ocean distances and for many years at a time. Therefore, although the Navy generally was going over to steam-alone propulsion, sail had to be the basic motive power of a sloop. As with HMS *Warrior*, the funnels were telescopic and the screw could be raised and lowered, to take account of the difference. When under sail alone, the screw was raised so as to avoid the drag of a large submerged surface, and the funnel or funnels lowered to avoid unnecessary wind resistance (as a funnel is a sail that cannot be furled), and to get them out of the way of the canvas sails. The order to change propulsion method from sail to steam was 'Up funnel, down screw'.

HMS *Gannet* in her heyday—at Suez in 1890. *Photo courtesy Keith Hallam, Borough of Gosport*

In construction, however, the *Gannet* was quite different from both the old wooden sailing warships and the new iron ones. She was of so-called 'composite' build—the framing of the hull, the skeleton, so to speak, was of iron, the skin of the ship was of teak. In this respect she was a rare specimen, as this method of construction lasted for only a few years.

The *Gannet*'s first patrol cruise was to South America but included visits to Hawaii and Tahiti. For the rest of her active service career along the trade routes of empire she was in the Eastern Mediterranean, the newly-cut Suez Canal, and the Red Sea. It was in the latter area, off the island of Suakin, that for the first time in her career real active service was logged, on 15 September, 1888:

06.20: Fired 3 shells, 5″ B.L., at Osman Digna's men behind the lines.

Osman Digna was the wiliest of the Dervish chiefs who took part in the Mahdist uprising—a fanatical Islamic movement which saw the death of General Gordon in 1885, the capture of Khartoum by Kitchener in 1898 after the battle of Omdurman (in which the young Winston Churchill took part), the death of the Khalifa in 1899 and at last, the last of them all, the capture of Osman Digna in 1900—the man whom the Sudanese called the 'Grand Master of the Art of Flight', because of his belief that a dead soldier was a bad soldier.

Gannet had returned to Malta to pay off in 1888. Her active career ended in 1895, at Sheerness. Stripped of her engines, she became a sail training ship in an age of steam. The broadside was no more; not, at least, in the form of scores of tiny guns. Now battleships were made of steel and carried a few really heavy guns in revolving turrets.

After becoming HMS *President*, moored in the Thames, the ex-*Gannet* was moved to the Hamble river near Southampton to take the place of another training ship, the worn-out barque *Mercury*, whose name she acquired and retained until the school closed down in 1968. Her decks had been built over to provide extra accommodation and she had no mast. In this form, after being taken over by the Maritime Trust, she was brought round to Portsmouth in the late 1970s, when a local society was formed at Gosport to preserve her. They worked regularly at weekends to remove a shed and other odd constructions dating from her training school years, in the hope that funds would become available to restore her fully.

The background to the battle which overtook these enthusiasts was the closing down completely of Chatham Dockyard and the progressive rundown of Portsmouth Dockyard to become just a maintenance and repair depot, with much of its labour force laid off.

Ripe for restoration: HMS *Gannet* in Portsmouth Harbour in 1985. A helicopter from the current HMS *Gannet* hovers overhead. *Photo courtesy Keith Hallam, Borough of Gosport*

(This was temporarily halted for the brief Falklands Conflict of 1982, when hundreds of men with dismissal notices in their pockets were called back to work.)

Gosport thought that they could employ some 70 of these skilled craftsmen in the restoration of HMS *Gannet*, and turn her into a tourist attraction as part of the naval package in the Portsmouth Harbour area, which now housed *Mary Rose* as well as HMS *Victory*, and would soon include HMS *Warrior*. Chatham at this time had no historic ships at all, although, like Portsmouth, it did have many historic dockyard buildings. The Gosport bid to the Maritime Trust, who owned her, was backed by Hampshire County Council as well; but Chatham conquered. No sooner had *Warrior* been towed in to Portsmouth in 1987 than *Gannet* was towed out.

Over the years there had been other bids; Greenwich and Woolwich had been interested; there was a possibility of a berth in St Katherine's Dock, London; and a number of marinas thought her a useful attraction. It was at least a welcome change from 1949, when a ship which had actually fired at HMS *Victory* at Trafalgar and seen battle under the British flag in the Baltic, was simply scuttled in deep water as an unnecessary nuisance. And yet all the *Gannet* could boast of was a few shots at Osman Digna's dervishes.

She is now undergoing restoration in No. 3 Dock as part of the Chatham Historic Dockyard project. The first dry dock to be made in England was completed at Portsmouth in 1496 by order of King Henry VII. Chatham began more modestly in 1547, with a rented storehouse for sails and rigging, used for refitting ships which were normally laid up each winter.* The first ship built at Chatham was the 25-ton pinnace *Sun*, which took part in the Armada campaign of 1588 (the *Moon*, at 35 tons, was larger). By the 1720s, when Daniel Defoe wrote his account, Chatham was a proper dockyard. It was here that HMS *Victory* was built during 1759-1765, and where Charles Dickens's father worked as a clerk in the pay office.

A dockyard is always a specialised industrial site and possesses some peculiar buildings. The old covered slipways, dating from 1836 to 1855, loom as large as cathedrals, while the rope-walk is 1,140 feet long and only 47 feet wide. And, of course, there are the giant 'warehouses' for ships' gear and the mast-ponds, contrasting with the gracious administration buildings. The largest ship built here was HMS *Africa*, a pre-Dreadnought battleship of 16,350 tons, in 1905; the last was a submarine for Canada in 1966. In 1984 it was over.

The problem was what to do with a large industrial and administration area no longer required, and the practical answers are still being worked out.

* The 1500-ton *Henry Grace de Dieu* ('Great Harry') was not built at Chatham but at Woolwich in 1514, a gigantic version of the successful *Mary Rose*.

Address
Chatham Historic Dockyard, Dock Road, Chatham, Kent, Telephone: (0634) 812551

Opening Times
1 April to 25 Oct, Wed-Sun and Bank holidays 10 am to 5 pm. Rest of year Wed, Sat, Sun, 10 am to 3.30 pm.

Entrance Fees
Guided tour: adults £2.75, children £1.50.
Unguided tour: adults £1.75, children £1.00.
Group rates:
Guided tour: adults £2.25, children £1.00.
Unguided tour: Adults £1.25, children 75p.
Children under 5 free.

Clock House and Dry Dock, Ramsgate

The restoration of the Clock House at Ramsgate's Royal Harbour began in 1982, and in 1984 the building was opened as a museum by the Prime Minister. The emphasis is on local events, because this south-eastern tip of England has an unusual history. 1,000 years ago the whole of Thanet was an island, separated from mainland Kent by the Wantsum Channel.

Ramsgate overlooks the Goodwin Sands, the dreaded 'ship swallower'. In one horrific storm, the Great Gale of 1703, no less then three battleships were lost there, together with most of their crews. One of them, probably the *Stirling Castle*, has been found and artefacts from her are exhibited in the museum.

In war, Ramsgate is a front-line town. In the Great War of 1914-18 the harbour was attacked both by Zeppelins and by Gothas, but most of the action took place out in the Channel, where U-boats tried to break through the barriers, and Ramsgate was a base for the Dover Patrol. On one occasion three drifters, crewed by fishermen, were out minesweeping when they saw U-48 laying mines; although these were fishing vessels, with tiny guns, they holed the submarine and, acting in concert, drove it on to the Goodwins. Early in the war the Germans sank HMS *Niger*, the Ramsgate guard ship.

The Clock House and Dry Dock at Ramsgate in about 1890. The former is now a maritime museum, and the restored dock displays historic vessels. *Photo: Ramsgate Marine Heritage*

Commander Lightoller's motor yacht *Sundowner*, photographed between the wars.

At the start of World War II, Ramsgate was a control point in the contraband service; large convoys of foreign merchant ships gathered there for examination. Then came Dunkirk, when 42,000 men of the defeated BEF passed through Ramsgate. When the Luftwaffe had established bases on the French coast, some 20 miles away, few convoys got through unscathed—some suffered 50 per cent losses when only a few miles off shore; and then, for weeks nothing moved on the waters. Air battles were an almost daily occurrence for more than three months, mixed with a little lethal shelling by heavy guns in France. In 1941 Ramsgate became a Coastal Forces base and in 1944 the port contributed to the invasion of Normandy. The museum reflects all these events.

In the dry dock is the motor yacht *Sundowner* which went to Dunkirk with a man and two boys (Commander Lightoller, a survivor of the *Titanic*, his son Roger and a Sea Scout called Gerald Ashcroft) and returned with 130. The yacht was built as an Admiralty launch in 1912 (also the year of the *Titanic*'s sinking); bought by Lightoller in 1929; and converted for family use, visiting such ports as Dunkirk, Ostend, Flushing, Boulogne, St Valery in peace time. In 1939 Lightoller (with his wife along for cover) made a secret survey of the German coast for the Admiralty—recalling the exploits of the *Dulcibella* as told in the 1903 thriller by Erskine Childers, *The Riddle of the Sands*. The photographs, maps and soundings from Lightoller's voyage were never put to active use.

Sundowner's most famous voyage began on 1 June, 1940. She had a registered tonnage of 26 tons, could make 10 knots on her 72 hp Gleniffer diesel, drew five feet of water, and her previous maximum number of passengers had been 21.

In the afternoon, having dodged Luftwaffe attacks by bomb and bullet in the morning, they came across the *Westerley* on fire and took off from her five survivors; they then carried on towards the beaches. They found that the soldiers were being taken off from the outer piers, which were too high for the yacht, so Lightoller came alongside the destroyer *Worchester* and embarked his cargo there. The first 75 men he sent below, making them lie down for stability reasons, and also jettisoning all their equipment, even their boots. Then he started packing more soldiers on deck. When the grand total, including his crew and the five from *Westerley*, had reached 130 and *Sundowner* was dangerously low in the water, Lightoller set off for Ramsgate, which they reached 12 hours after leaving there that morning. The soldiers started to move before they were told to do so—and *Sundowner* almost capsized before Lightoller could regain control. In that one-half of a June day in 1940 *Sundowner* saw more action than many warships did in the whole of their careers.

Also exhibited at the dock is the 233-ton steam tug *Cervia*, built in 1946 to a Government design for supporting vessels intended for the Normandy invasion and after. Her career in towing and salvage work was briefly halted in 1954 when she sank off Tilbury Docks, in

The steam tug *Cervia. Photo: Maritime Museum Ramsgate*

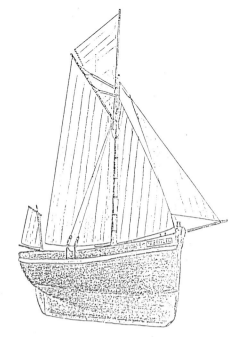

The South Devon fishing smack *Vanessa*, 1899.

a tragic accident which took the lives of her captain and four of her crew.

Another vessel on view is the South Devon fishing smack *Vanessa* of 1899, very similar to those used at Ramsgate.

How to Get There
Follow signs for the Royal Harbour, which is surrounded by a number of historic buildings. Further along the coast, at Broadstairs, is the house once owned by Charles Dickens, whose preserved desk directly overlooks the Channel (for his birthplace you have to go to Portsmouth).

Address
East Kent Maritime Trust, Maritime Museum, The Clockhouse, Pier Yard, Royal Harbour, Ramsgate, Kent, CT11 8LS.
Telephone: (0843) 587765

Opening Times
April to September: Mon to Fri 11 am to 4 pm. Sat to Sun 2 to 5 pm
October to March: Mon to Fri 11 am-3.30 pm.

Entrance Fees
There are admission charges with a reduction for children and OAPs. Groups and schools by arrangement.

SS *Great Britain*: 'A Dead Mouse' from the Falklands

HISTORY

Floated out of dock at Bristol	1843
First Liverpool-New York passage	1845
Stranded in Northern Ireland	1846
Salvaged	1847
Sold to Gibbs, Bright	1850
Re-engined and rig altered	1851-2
First Australian passage (Gold Rush)	1852
Run in conjunction with *Royal Charter*	1855-9
Troopship for Crimean War	1856
Troopship for Indian Mutiny	1857
Sold and turned into a sailing ship	1882
Damaged off Cape Horn and abandoned in Falklands	1886
Used for storing wool and coal until	1933
Scuttled in Sparrow Cove, Falklands	1937
Great Britain Project set up and survey made	1968
Salvaged and returned to original dock in Bristol	1970

SPECIFICATIONS

Length	for tonnage 83.5m (274 ft); upper deck 94m (308 ft); overall 98m (322 ft)
Breadth	for tonnage 14.7m (48 ft 2 ins); overall 15.5m (51 ft)
Depth of Hold	9.6m (31 ft 6 ins). Laden draught 4.9m (16 ft)
Tonnage	2936 gross; 1017 net; by old measurement 2443 tons
Capacity	360 passengers, in 28 staterooms with single berths and 113 with two. Crew 130. Cargo 1,200 tons Bunkers 1000-1200 tons
Engines	Geared type, 4 cylinders in two pairs. Weight 340 tons
Boilers	One assembly 10.4m (34 ft) long, 9.4m (31 ft) wide, 6.6m (21½ ft) high. Weight 200 tons.

Screw	Six bladed, 4.7m (15½ ft) diameter. Weight 4 tons.
Rig	Six masts. The main mast only had yards and 'square' sails, and was fixed. The others, with 'fore & aft' rig, were hinged for lowering.

Dr Ewen Corlett, the naval architect who was responsible for the technical decisions made in the return of the ship from the Falklands, recently summed up the importance of the *Great Britain* as 'the first large commercial ship, the first ocean-going metal ship, the first ocean-going screw propelled ship and the first ship to introduce a whole range of complex modern features purely because by then they existed to be used and could be with advantage.'

The dominating genius behind her design and construction was Isambard Brunel, an all-round engineer who designed not only ships but tunnels, railways, bridges, docks and harbours. A contemporary writer declared: 'This wonderful vessel will combine a greater number of varieties and untried principles than ever before united in one enterprise.'

The SS *Great Britain* in dock at Bristol, April 1971, soon after being towed back from the Falklands on a submersible pontoon. *Photo: Alexander McKee*

The clipper-type bow of the *Great Britain* (*left*) and her over-hanging stern. *Photos: Alexander McKee*

These innovations included, apart from an iron hull and a screw propeller, which other smaller vessels possessed, such totally new features as a six-bladed propeller, a semi-balanced rudder, wire rigging, an electric log, a double bottom, transverse watertight bulkheads, folding masts, and a hollow wrought-iron propeller shaft. The great size of the ship, made possible by the Industrial Revolution, should enable her to carry sufficient coal for a complete Atlantic crossing; and the iron construction should avoid the drawback to putting engines into a wooden ship—they caused the hull to sag in the middle under the weight.

What was not foreseen was the timidity of the travelling public and of businessmen generally. On her first transatlantic passage she carried few passengers (variously reported as 45 or 60) and only 600 tons of cargo. Nevertheless, the *Great Britain* made New York, 3,300 miles away, in just under 15 days at an average speed of about $9\frac{1}{2}$ knots (rather more than 10 mph), to tremendous press notices. The *New York Herald* announced:

The monster of the deep, a sort of mastodon of this age, the *Great Britain*, arrived on Sunday afternoon, the 10th (of

August, 1845). The announcement threw the city into a state of great excitement and thousands rushed to the Battery, to the wharves on the East River, to the Brooklyn Heights, and to the Atlantic Steamship Pier at the foot of Clinton Street, to get a sight of her . . . This magnificent steamer came up the Bay in beautiful style. The great problem whether or not a steamer of the magnitude and construction of the *Great Britain*, and incorporating her principle of propulsion, could make a successful trip across the ocean, is now satisfactorily and happily solved.

She made faster passages later on, in 13½ days from Liverpool to New York, but, because of the Australian Gold Rush of the 1850s, spent more of her career on the Australian route, which she ran in conjunction with the newer but slightly smaller *Royal Charter*, so that they might almost be called 'liners' in the sense of ships running regularly to a time-table, like trains. Launched in 1855 and from the same stable which had produced the *Great Britain* (the builder of both ships was William Patterson), the *Royal Charter* could make 14½ knots under sail alone and touched 18 knots under steam and sail. Their partnership lasted until the winter of 1859, when the *Royal Charter* was destroyed by a hurricane on the coast of Anglesey.*

HMS *Warrior* of 1860 owed a great deal to Brunel's example with the SS *Great Britain*, and to the industrial base which made them possible; and it is curious that both these revolutionary ships, which marked decisive development stages in the warship and the commercial vessel, should have been fortunately preserved by a series of happenings, most of which were accidental.

The Falklands was a graveyard of sailing ships which had failed to round Cape Horn and retired, damaged, to their last haven; the *Great Britain* was merely one of seventeen. However, in 1966, the Pacific Bridge and Engineering Company of San Francisco decided that this particular ship might be worth saving; but on learning of the British project very generously waived their claim.

The British millionaire, Jack Hayward, put up £150,000 and the project could mount their survey. During the time the ship had been used as a wool store, an entry port had been cut in her side, and after thirty-odd years of neglect this had started a seven-inch crack in the hull; numerous holes had been cut below the waterline to destroy her buoyancy; the iron hull plates had wasted to nearly 50 per cent of their original thickness: and much of the decking had disappeared.

* See *The Golden Wreck* by Alexander McKee (Souvenir Press, 1961 and 1986).

In her final years the *Great Britain* reverted to sail only and her engines were removed. This view of her rudder, however, shows the end of the propeller shaft still visible.
Photo: Alexander McKee.

The Great Britain's 'tumble-home' amidships.
Photo: Alexander McKee

The ship is re-masted. *Photo: Ilse McKee*

The original plan, to fill the hull with plastic foam or buoyancy bags, had to be dropped. The salvors, Risdon Beazley of Southampton and Ulrich Harms of Hamburg, proposed instead that the *Great Britain* be refloated and then 'beached' on top of a submersible pontoon; and that, perched on the now risen pontoon, she should make the long tow back to England. This was done.

The result was consternation in Bristol, where the tow was to end. Admiral Sir Patrick Bayly, head of the Maritime Trust, recalled recently: 'There is a story that when the Leader of the Bristol City Council was shown the *Great Britain* he said: "You are like a cat who drops a dead mouse at our feet and expects us to admire it." '

In my own file on the project, I have a number of clippings from the *Sunday Telegraph* in 1971. 'UP BRISTOL'S CREEK WITHOUT A PADDLE', ran one cruel headline, followed by a comment that 'Bristol Corporation, in a crescendo of apathy, also decided not to make any grant towards restoration, nor to provide any parking facilities. They have even refused planning permission to dig a drain to take slops from a temporary canteen.' This earned a reply from Alderman Marcus Hartnell of Bristol, who asked of the journalist:

Is he aware that the SS *Great Britain* was possibly the most unlucky ship ever launched in Bristol, and certainly a financial disaster? . . . Can you wonder then, that the Bristol Corporation looks doubtfully at this unfortunate relic, which well-meaning people have towed up and left in our river? We must be thankful that no one has, as yet, dumped a Bristol Bulldog Fighter on College Green, and suggested we restore that!

While the Alderman had a point regarding the cost of restoration of ships, he was all at sea regarding aircraft. At a time when a Spitfire is worth its weight in gold, a Bristol Bulldog would surely weigh-in in diamonds!

The *Great Britain* in process of restoration at Bristol. *Photo courtesy SS Great Britain Trading Ltd*

By October of 1971 Portsmouth Corporation were bidding to take the *Great Britain* off Bristol's uncertain hands, on the grounds that Isambard Brunel was a Portsmouth man, and one Councillor (who surely needed a tape measure) proposed that she be put in Long Curtain Battery Moat with HMS *Victory*, to be relocated there. This sparked a furious reply from 'Watchdog' of Paulsgrove:

As a ratepayer, I am incensed by the negotiations under way for Portsmouth Corporation to have a hulk—the steamship *Great Britain*—berthed here at heavy cost. As I see it, this would simply add more junk to an already depressed-looking area.

'Watchdog's' wishes were fulfilled and in 1975 the Portsmouth *Evening News* sighed:

The day Portsmouth lost out to Bristol in the bid to provide a permanent home for SS *Great Britain* was one where Portsmouth literally and metaphorically missed the boat. Apart from losing a source of revenue, Portsmouth lost a priceless addition to the nucleus of a maritime museum.

Who was right? Almost everyone, actually. Until the last week of November 1987, only the clipper *Cutty Sark* at Greenwich was making a profit, out of all the historic ships preserved in Great Britain. Since then, however, the *Mary Rose* has started to pay her way, with 360,000 visitors and the Trust's once enormous overdraft wiped out at last.

It is not, however, merely a question of whether or not the ship pays for itself, but its value to the area as a general tourist attraction. Portsmouth, formerly a great naval and military base, languished when Britain ceased to have an Empire and to support huge fleets; a great deal of its future prosperity does now lie with tourism.

The cost is of course a continuing one. On the *Great Britain* restoration work has progressed to the point where the promenade saloon is being fitted out and installation of the main engine frame is underway. When completed, the engine will be a full working replica; the work should be completed by 1991.

How to Get There
Map in brochure. By bus, City Badger No. 511 from City Centre and Bus Station. The Ship is signposted throughout the City and there is a car and coach park. Entrance is through the Maritime Heritage Centre.

Address
SS Great Britain, Great Western Dock, Gas Ferry Road (off Cumberland Road), Bristol.
Telephone: (0272) 260680.

Opening Times
Daily (including Sunday but excluding 24th and 25th December):
10 am to 6 pm (Summer).
10 am to 5 pm (Winter).

Entrance Fees
Adults £1.70, OAPs and children under 16, 80p, children under 5 free. Special rates for schools and parties.

Exeter Maritime Museum: 'The World's Premier Boat Museum'

Also known as the 'PLEASE TOUCH MUSEUM', because visitors and their children are invited to make themselves at home (while exercising reasonable care not to fall overboard or into engine-rooms) the Exeter Maritime Museum stocks a supply of working vessels, small craft and boats gathered from all over the world.

Exeter was an inland port in the time of the Romans (and probably long before that), although the canal was dug more recently (in 1566) and the dock area around it is more recent still. But in 1963 all this was becoming derelict. Now hundreds of craft are to be seen tied up alongside in the basin, standing on the quayside or in buildings fronting it.

The range of boats displayed is very wide. At one end of the range

Beautifully painted Portuguese fishing boat.
Photo: Alexander McKee

The Tagus lighter *Sotero*, another wonderful example of decorative painting. *Photo: Ilse McKee*

is the world's oldest working steamboat: Brunel's drag-boat, built for clearing mud from Bridgwater Dock in Somerset in 1844 (a year after the launch of the *Great Britain*). Unlovely but useful, it contrasts with the strikingly beautiful paintwork of the Portuguese boats which are almost surrealist in shape. The high-curved ends of the latter, similar to Minoan craft extinct for thousands of years, probably served the function of the roll-over bars on some motor vehicles, because they are designed to be beach-launched with 44 men on board, by a beach party of 15 more men and 20 oxen. Their purpose is to catch sardines, launching from and returning to particular beaches in particular conditions.

This is why almost every boat is different, although sometimes economic or social factors affect design. The Arab dhow, for instance, has an extremely powerful and efficient lateen rig (probably copied by the great European explorers), which requires a large crew to handle it and is best for long ocean voyages in steady wind conditions, while the Thames barge is designed for a crew of two, in an area where the cost of labour is high.

There is good reason for all the many differences. For instance,

The Hong Kong fishing trawler *Ha Kau*.
Photo: Ilse McKee

The Danish steam tug *St Canute* (*ex-St Knut*).
Photo: Alexander McKee

Expert workmanship in a shallow boat of bound reeds.
Photo: Alexander McKee

Fijian and other 'native' craft seem to have upside down sails, with more canvas at the top than at the bottom. This is because the wind is moving faster higher up the mast than it is lower down near the interaction with the water surface. But this rig is used in conjunction either with a double-hull or outrigger, which does not heel much. The European monohull is not symmetrical when heeled and therefore loses efficiency. Also, it is not nearly so fail-safe; whereas the South Seas craft will continue to float even if swamped, a modern monohull (like the old sailing ships) is heavily ballasted. The whole museum is thought-provoking and some of its craft are still sailed, so as to preserve something of the techniques of actually handling them to best advantage.

How to Get There
By car, head for City Centre and look for Maritime Museum signs. There is ample car parking by the museum. The nearest railway station is Exeter St Davids.

Address
International Sailing Craft Association, The Quay, Exeter, Devon, EX2 4AN. Telephone: (0392) 58075

Opening Times
Every day except Christmas Day and Boxing Day:
October to May: 10 am to 5 pm.
June-September: 10 am to 6 pm.
Evening visits by arrangement.

Entrance Fees
Adults £2.80, children £1.50, OAPs £2.50.
Family ticket £7.50.
How-to-get-there map in brochure.

---

5 THE LONDON AREA

The Clipper *Cutty Sark*: The Most Profitable Ship

HISTORY

Launched at Dumbarton, Scotland	1869
Suez Canal opened	1869
Eight Tea Trade voyages to Shanghai or Woosung	1870–7
Coal, Scrap-iron and General cargoes	1878–83
Wool Trade to Australia	1883–95
Under Portuguese flag	1895–1922
Bought by Captain Dowman and restored	1922–4
Exhibited during Festival of Britain	1951
Moved to purpose-built dock at Greenwich	1954
Formally opened by HM The Queen and Prince Philip	1957
$10\frac{1}{2}$ million visitors logged in 30 years	1987

SPECIFICATIONS

Length overall	85.3m (280 ft)
Length between perpendiculars	64.8m (212 ft 6 ins)
Beam	11m (36 ft)
Depth (moulded)	6.9m (22 ft 6 ins)
Gross tonnage	963 tons
Net tonnage	921 tons
Displacement at 20 ft draught	2,100 tons
Sail area	2972.8 sq m (32,000 sq ft)

Until 1987 the *Cutty Sark*, with 375,000 visitors, was the only historic ship in Britain to pay her way, but in that year the *Mary Rose* began to catch up, with 360,000. HMS *Victory* lay third at 326,000 and still making a loss, followed, it is estimated, by HMS *Belfast* (with much work needing to be done on her), the *Great Britain*, HMS *Warrior* (but with figures only for the period August to October, so she will do much better in 1988), HMS *Alliance* neck-and-neck with Exeter Maritime Museum, the *Discovery*, *Gipsy Moth IV*, and the *Kathleen & May*. In all, a probable total of two million visitors a year, not counting the many other ship and boat museums which have recently come into being, and others which will soon be active.

A boat on the clipper's deck stands out against the intricate pattern of standing and running rigging. *Photo: Alexander McKee*

A notable failure was HMS *Cavalier* which, having failed at Southampton, failed again at Brighton and has now gone up north to Tyne and Wear. In this case, it must be said, the sites available were not conducive to public visiting. Shoreside berths, like moorings, are at a premium, particularly for largish vessels. Ship-parking anywhere can be just as difficult as car parking in large cities.

Greenwich has certainly proved to be an inspired site for the *Cutty Sark* which, although a Scottish ship, often used the Thames during her varied career. Greenwich is the pleasantly landscaped home of the National Maritime Museum, the Royal Naval College and, for many years, the Royal Observatory, and is within easy reach by public transport of the centre of London and its inexhaustible reservoir of visitors. Car parking, once easy, is becoming increasingly difficult, although still not impossible.

The ship herself was ordered in a fit of rivalry by a Scottish shipowner who wanted to win one of the famous tea races; and just to rub it in, if he won, named her after a piece of provocative underwear worn by a beautiful young witch in a ballad by 'Rabbie' Burns. At *her* coven the Devil played the bagpipes.

The clipper *Cutty Sark*, Britain's most popular historic ship. *Photo: Alexander McKee*

The figurehead of the *Cutty Sark* portrays the young witch 'Nannie' who, in Robert Burns' famous poem, pursued Tam O'Shanter dressed only in her shift and came close enough to tear off his horse's tail. *Photo: Alexander McKee*

The clipper type has been compared to Concorde—very fast, very expensive, highly specialised. They were built for trades where speed paid off, so they were ocean racers: first in bringing home the tea from China (for the faster the ship the fresher the tea and the better the prices the owner got); and also, when the Australian gold rush began, first in carrying passengers. As speed is partly a matter of waterline length, they were built long and narrow; and because the higher you get the faster the wind, they had tall masts. And because commercial pressures were sharp—and the opening of the Suez Canal, which favoured the steamer, made them sharper—their captains tended to be successful 'drivers', both of ships and of men. The *Cutty Sark* was launched just a little late to be really successful and although a good ship, she was not, alas for her owner, John Willis, a truly outstanding vessel. However, she is the only surviving preserved ship of her type.

Of the great North American clippers, only one remains—but as a wreck. This is the *Snow Squall*, built at Cape Elizabeth, Maine, in 1851, and abandoned in the Falklands in 1864. Although lying in

Two examples from the collection of figureheads displayed in the hold of the *Cutty Sark. Photos: Alexander McKee*

Port Stanley Harbour, she survived the conflict of 1982; and American marine archaeologists have plans for recovering what still remains of the hull.

The *Cutty Sark* is one of many vessels owned by the Maritime Trust, and chartered to other organisations better positioned to fund and care for them. They own another Greenwich exhibit, Sir Francis Chichester's ketch *Gipsy Moth IV* of 1966; and also, down at Portsmouth, almost alongside *Warrior*, Sir Alec Rose's ketch *Lively Lady* of 1948. Both of them are solo-round-the-world craft, their tiny size making the feat more remarkable.

Until 1986 the Trust had a number of vessels in the London area concentrated in St Katherine's Dock by the Tower. But these had to be dispersed and a new home in an off-Thames dock by Southwark Cathedral was found for the *Kathleen & May*, a schooner of 1900, which can easily be reached by public transport. Built near Chester, she was employed in the coasting and short sea trades to carry cargoes of coal, cement, pitch, clay, pit-props and so on. She is 98 feet long with a gross tonnage of 136 and a cargo capacity of 226 tons: a vessel of a type which was typical of local sea transport for many centuries and has only been phased out in quite modern times.

The collection of vessels, boats and barges remaining in St Katherine's Dock include (at the time of writing, for it is a floating population in more ways than one) the red-painted Nore Light Vessel, built in 1931 in the Isle of Wight, and the steam tug *Challenge*, built the same year in Scotland for work on the Thames. She is 100 feet long and of 212 tons. There are also many sailing barges among the craft moored in the modern marina-cum-shopping arcade-cum-harbourside café area which has arisen on the war-damaged, semi-derelict dockland, and transformed it into a peaceful water oasis in the centre of roaring London. Indeed, the site originally was that of the Hospice of St Katherine, founded in 1146. This and the surrounding 1,250 houses were demolished in 1824 to provide 25 acres of docks which, by 1966, were outmoded. There were no little schooners and barques any more; instead giant container ships and tankers so large that they look like the Isle of Wight on the move, draw 50 to 70 feet of water, and can be measured by the half-mile rather than the foot. As most of the craft now in the dock are privately owned, it is a case of Look—but Don't Touch.

Close by the *Cutty Sark* is displayed Sir Francis Chicherster's ketch *Gipsy Moth IV*. Photo: *Alexander McKee*

(Left) the schooner *Kathleen & May*, 1900, at her berth in St Mary Overy Dock at Southwark. *Photo: Teresa Watkins.* (*Right*) the Nore Light vessel at St Katherine's Dock. *Photo: Alexander McKee*

Address
Clipper Ship *Cutty Sark*, King William Walk, Greenwich, London, SE10 9BL.
Telephone: Ship: 01-858 3445. Bookings: 01-853 3589

Opening Times
Mon–Sat 10 am to 6 pm, Sun 12.00 to 6 pm (March to October).
Mon–Sat 10 am to 5 pm, Sun 12.00 to 5 pm (November to February).

Entrance Fees
Adults £1.30, 70p for under-16's and OAPs.
Prebooked parties of 15 or more: adults 80p, 40p for under-16s (except Bank Holidays).

Gipsy Moth IV, close by, is open only in summer, at 20p for adults, 10p for under-16s.

HMS *Belfast*: 'Why Not This One?'

HISTORY

Class	Modified *Southampton* class
Built	Harland & Wolff, Belfast
Keel laid	December 1936
Launched	March 1938
Commissioned	August 1939

SPECIFICATIONS

Standard Displacement	10,553 tons
Overall Length	187m (613 ft 6 ins)
Breadth	20m (66 ft)
Draught	5.3m (17 ft 3 ins)
Engines	Parsons turbines driving 4 shafts. 80,000 ship horsepower giving 32 knots.
Complement	750–850 officers and men
Sister Ship	HMS *Edinburgh* (sunk May 1942)

ARMAMENT (1939)

Twelve 6-in guns in four turrets with a range of 14 miles and a possible rate of fire of 96 rounds per minute from all four turrets.
Twelve 4-in QF guns in six twin high-angle low-angle mountings as secondary and AA armament.
Sixteen 2-pdr pom-poms in 8-barrelled mountings and eight .5-in machine-guns as close-in AA defence.
Six 21-inch torpedoes in two triple tubes.
Two aircraft.

Vice-Admiral Sir Patrick Bayly, chairman of the Maritime Trust, recalls that when, in 1967, there was a museum-backed demand for a cruiser to preserve and exhibit, those concerned were invited down to Portsmouth and given lunch in the cruiser *Belfast*, which was then flagship of the Reserve Fleet. So someone asked suddenly: 'Why not this one?' *Belfast* certainly had the necessary battle honours, and must soon be due for the scrapyard. Admiral Sir Morgan Giles took charge, John Smith once again came up with an offer of a substantial sum of money (£100,000) and Lord Louis Mountbatten gave his

HMS *Belfast* at her anchorage near Tower Bridge. *Photo: Ilse McKee*

backing and help to seek further funding. One day, when I was leading the *Mary Rose* diving team out to Spithead in Tony Glover's trawler (herself a converted lifeboat from the *Queen Mary*), we saw that *Belfast* was on the move under the guidance of tugs, off on her final trip to the Thames, where she would be moored in view of Tower Hill. That was in September 1971, and our own enterprise was barely credible, although Lord Mountbatten and the Duke of Edinburgh both supported it. When, shortly afterwards, Lord Mountbatten was murdered by the IRA, the loss of such an important backer put the *Belfast* in trouble. A great deal now needs doing on the upper deck, but even so, the ship is well worth a visit, bringing to life much that one has read about Second World War battles at sea.

As a schoolboy in the 1930s, I had fairly free run over warships, particularly when my father was in the then flagship of the Reserve Fleet, the light cruiser *Centaur*, the rest of the 'fleet' consisting of four V & W class destroyers. These were essentially Jutland-style ships, whereas the *Belfast* was not merely larger than an equivalent 1914–18 ship but was packed with radar and other high-tech gadgetry vital to the new style warfare, and also with AA guns of all types, keys to survival in the conditions of 1939–45.

The *Belfast* was one of the very first casualties of the war. Soon after capturing the German liner *Cap Norte* while on northern patrol during October 1939, she set off one of the new magnetic mines which caused major hull fractures, unlike the horned and moored 'contact' mines of World War I. Her back was broken. She was out of action until December 1942. This was the period of the hard-fought Arctic convoys to Murmansk in North Russia, which were threatened not only by aircraft and submarines but by German battleships and battlecruisers based on the Norwegian fjords. Towards the end of December 1943, a trap was laid, using a convoy to lure out the 32,000-ton *Scharnhorst* (nine 11-inch and twelve 5.9 inch guns) to attack it while two British forces, led by the new battleship *Duke of York* (with ten 14-inch guns as her main armament), formed the two prongs of the ambush.

Force One was led by Vice-Admiral Burnett in *Belfast*, accompanied by two other cruisers, *Sheffield* and *Norfolk*. *Belfast* had been virtually reconstructed and had a changed armament and the latest radar and radio gear; and was in fact more formidable than she had been in 1939, although at a cost in speed of two knots. Force Two, under Admiral Fraser in *Duke of York*, consisted of one more cruiser, the *Jamaica*, and four destroyers initially.

The *Belfast*'s formidable array of guns in her after turrets. *Photo: Alexander McKee*

Six-inch gun turret (*left*) and the bridge behind, and (*right*) 40mm Bofors. *Photos: Alexander McKee*

The manoeuvres were long and complicated, carried out in the bitter cold and darkness of the Arctic winter. The chances of survival in the water were small for the men of any defeated ship.

Belfast's radar was the first to pick up the 'blip' which was the *Scharnhorst*. It was the day after Christmas. Contact was lost for some hours and then regained by *Belfast*. Shortly after, she lit up *Scharnhorst* with starshell and all three cruisers of Force One opened fire at 10,500 yards, and continued firing for 20 minutes, scoring hits but doing no significant damage. Knowing that Force Two was on a course to intercept ahead, Burnett kept tracking the *Scharnhorst* by radar; but both *Norfolk* and *Sheffield* had to reduce speed, leaving only *Belfast* to track and hold on to the dangerous quarry. Within minutes *Scharnhorst* was also on *Duke of York*'s radar.

Scharnhorst, twisting and turning, hit time after time, and finally with all her turrets knocked out and speed reduced, was still trying to escape. She was hit repeatedly, not only by the battleship but also by the circling cruisers; and was finally despatched by torpedoes from the destroyers. When *Belfast* was sent in to finish her off, also with torpedoes, she found nothing remaining on the surface of the sea but two small groups of German sailors on rafts—one group of 30, the other of six—all who were still alive out of the 1,968 men of her crew. Not a single officer was among the fortunate, gallant 36.

Among many other actions in northern waters, the *Belfast* took part in a large operation with aircraft carriers and battleships to destroy the German super-battleship *Tirpitz* in Altenfjord, Norway; 14 bombs hit *Tirpitz* and she was out of action for another three months.

Then came the invasion of Normandy, where *Belfast* served as bombardment ship for Third Canadian Infantry Division assaulting Juno beach near Courseulles and during its advance inland. The cruiser had not only taken part in the last action between British and German capital ships but assisted at the greatest seaborne invasion in history.

Refitted and modified once more for the war against Japan, the *Belfast* arrived in the Far East only after the surrender, but was sent out again from England in 1948, because of the fighting going on in Malaya and China, and was there when the Korean War broke out in 1950. For some two years she served as a shore bombardment ship; she fired more than 8,000 6-inch shells but was herself hit only once, with one man killed and four wounded.

How to Get There
Car parking is virtually impossible, but she is within easy walking distance of two tube stations—Tower Hill, north of the river (in summer there is a ferry service directly to *Belfast*), and London Bridge, south of the river.

Address
HMS *Belfast*, Symons Wharf, Vine Lane, Tooley Street, London SE1 2JA. Telephone: 01-407 6434.

Opening Times
Every day except the Christmas period:
11 am to 5.40 pm (April to October).
11 am to 4.30 pm (November to March).

Entrance Fees
Adults £3.00, OAPs and children £1.50.
Special rates for parties of more than ten.

---

6 SOUTH WALES

RNLB *Watkins Williams*: The VC's Lifeboat

SPECIFICATIONS

Length	12.8m (42 ft)
Beam	3.7m (12 ft)
Engines	Twin Gardner 48 hp diesels
Displacement	17 tons 6 cwt
Crew	7
Speed	8.5 knots
Cost when built	£27,801

The Welsh Industrial and Maritime Museum opened its first stage in 1977, making use of Cardiff docks—once great exporters of Welsh

Sketch of the lifeboat *Watkins Williams*.

Coxswain Richard Evans at the wheel of the *Watkins Williams*, which he used in the *Nafsiporos* rescue. *Photo courtesy RNLI*

coal but now, in common with most other such large complexes in Britain, fallen on hard times. So far, three vessels have been acquired, of which the most famous is the 42 ft Watson class lifeboat *Watkins Williams*, built in 1956 at a cost of £27,801. Between then and 1983, she was launched 154 times and saved 143 lives.

Her first years of service were at Moelfre on the north coast of Anglesey under a famous coxswain, Richard Evans, who had won his first 'lifeboat VC' (the RNLI Gold Medal) at the wreck of the steamer *Hindlea* in October, 1959, only a short distance from the remains of the *Royal Charter* and in the same conditions of 100 mph-plus winds. He made this rescue in the reserve lifeboat, *Edmund and Mary Robinson*.

He again won the Gold Medal in December, 1966, in the more modern *Watkins Williams*, in hurricane-force winds driving waves 35 feet high—nearly as high as his lifeboat was long. She was 42 feet with a 12 ft beam, displacing 17 tons 6 cwt. Her twin Gardner 48 hp diesels gave her a speed of $8\frac{1}{2}$ knots, which is about all that is practical in gale conditions. Her crew numbered seven.

In this case, the vessel in trouble, the Greek motor ship *Nafsiporos*, had not actually struck but was some 400 yards off the shore and being roughly treated by the tumultuous seas, her propeller lifting clear of the water. Even approaching such a hulk in such seas is highly dangerous, and the Moelfre lifeboat was damaged when the distressed vessel's own lifeboat crashed down onto her. Nevertheless, Dick Evans drove in and took off ten men from the Greek ship, while lifeboat and motor vessel rose and fell in that tremendous sea. For extreme skill, as well as great courage, never was a Gold Medal better earned.

Also on exhibition are the steam tug *Sea Alarm* of 1941, and the Bristol Channel pilot cutter *Kindly Light*, built in 1911.

Address
Welsh Industrial and Maritime Museum, Bute Street, Cardiff.
Telephone: (0222) 481919

Opening Times
Open: Tues to Sat 10 am to 5 pm; Sun 2.30 to 5 pm.
Closed: Mondays, Christmas Eve, Christmas Day, Boxing Day, New Year's Day, Good Friday, May Day.

Entrance Fees
Admission free with ample free coach and car parking.

---

7 THE NORTH WEST

The Boat Museum, Ellesmere Port: Inland Waterways

The idea for a National Waterways Museum dates from 1970 and the site eventually chosen was the derelict Shropshire Union Canal Basin at Ellesmere Port, south of Liverpool, near the junction of many motorways. It possessed water and quayside space for a large boat collection, together with traditional buildings which could be converted to workshops and an exhibition hall. The museum opened in June, 1976. Its object was not merely to collect the various types of craft used for inland navigation on canals and rivers but to try to create, for those with imagination, the life lived aboard them when they were part of the industrial scene. The Introduction to the Museum's booklet explains:

> If you look at the boats merely as exhibits it is difficult to imagine that people were born, reared, worked and died in them . . . Imagine that you drive a long-distance lorry and live in it with your family. You have no other home and you may or may not own the lorry. To eke out a living you and your family must assist with the driving, loading and unloading. You may make long journeys right across the country or short ones, within a confined area. Now, instead of a lorry, imagine that you all live in a small cabin about 6 feet by 8 feet at the end of a boat which you have to navigate with its cargo along the canals and that each one of you must work from dawn to dusk. The family must be dressed and fed, the horse or engine has to be fuelled and watered, cajoled and led; you have to manipulate the locks, swing-bridges, sluices, and cranes. The cargo must be delivered as soon as possible, whatever the weather. In the confined space of your cabin there is a place for everything and everything must be in its place. The cabin range must be kept warm all the year round for it is your only method of heating and cooking. In spite of the soot and ashes and the dirty cargo, you are expected to keep the boat, your clothes and yourself clean. If you are the wife you must also cook the meals, control

the children, steer the boat, and work the ropes. You cannot afford to be ill, you will probably never learn to read or write but you will develop an unfailing memory for accurate detail.

Not all families lived on their boats. Some of the larger, wider barges were crewed by men who lived in cottages on the banks of the canals and worked the boats only in daylight or for short distances, transferring their gear to another boat which they would bring back.

The boats (really barges) in the collection are of many types, narrow and wide, powered and unpowered, made of wood, of steel, or of composite construction—even (as a wartime measure) of concrete. There are Day Boats used for carrying coal in boxes—the earliest form of containerisation; there are tugs and ice-breakers and weed-cutters. By 1987 there were more than 60 of them.

How to Get There
Situated by Junction 9 of the M53, 15 minutes by car from Chester. Ellesmere Port Railway Station is five minutes' walk away. C3 buses from Chester and Birkenhead pass close by. Ample free car and coach parking.

Address
The Boat Museum, Dockyard Road, Ellesmere Port, Cheshire, L65 4ET. Telephone: 051-355 5017

Opening Times
April to October: 10 am to 5 pm every day; evenings by arrangement.
November to March: 11 am to 4 pm Sat to Thurs inclusive.

Entrance Fees
Adults £2.50, children £1.40, OAPs and students £1.80.
Family ticket £7.00.
Boat trips: Adults and OAPs £1, children 60p.
Boat charter: £100 for 3 hours.

Merseyside Maritime Museum, Liverpool

In Liverpool, as in so many ports, the extensive dock area has been

The colourful display of canal barges at the Boat Museum, Ellesmere Port. *Photo courtesy National Waterways Museum*

converted to modern leisure uses. Some Victorian buildings have been restored and the collection of vessels includes the schooner *De Wadden* of 1917, the Weaver packet *Wincham* of 1946, the pilot boat *Edmund Gardner* and the Mersey flat *Oakdale*, both built in 1953.

The museum houses relics washed ashore from the terrible *Royal Charter* wreck at Moelfre in Anglesey in 1859, including a wooden carving and a useless lifebelt. On that dreadful night of hurricane, few drowned: most were hammered and gashed to death on the rock ledges. Enquiries to: Merseyside Maritime Museum, Pier Head, Liverpool L3 1DN. Telephone: 051-236 1492.

Peggy: The Walled-Up Schooner

At Castletown in the Isle of Man there is an extraordinary survival of a rather ordinary craft. The *Peggy* was a schooner-rigged yacht which did double service, both as a pleasure craft for the owners and as a working yacht for local trading and fishing. She measured 8m

Merseyside Maritime Museum—Liverpool's dockland transformed. *Photo: Alexander McKee*

Relics displayed at the museum, taken from the wreck of the *Royal Charter*, a similar ship to the *Great Britain* (see p.66). She was only a few miles from her home port of Liverpool when she was driven onto the rocks off Anglesey in October 1859. *Photo: Alexander McKee*

(26 ft 5 in) overall, with a 2.3m (7 ft 8 ins) beam and an inside depth of 1.2m (4 ft)—that is, the size of the average craft used for diving off Portsmouth during the last 30 years. Few of these were specially built for divers and soon no record of them will remain; then, in 200 years from now, interest will be kindled and great controversy will arise about the nature of these 'diving boats', with all the participants unconsciously trying to tidy up what was in fact a chaotic situation, with little uniformity.

The *Peggy* was built in 1791 for Captain George Quayle, member of a rich and influential Manx family. His boathouse was enlarged to accommodate her, and when she reached the end of her useful life, she was walled up and the dock enclosing her filled in, thus almost perfectly preserving an ordinary local craft of the time. It was her very ordinariness which made her important—vessels like this are often poorly recorded, if at all, precisely because they are so commonplace. For a century the existence of *Peggy* in her walled-up boat cellar was almost forgotten: then in 1935 she was 'rediscovered', and eventually became the nucleus of the expanding Nautical Museum at Castletown. This is closed in the winter, and enquiries are best made to The Manx Museum, Douglas, Isle of Man. Telephone: (0624) 75522.

HMS *Cavalier:* 'The Greyhound'

HISTORY

Class	Greyhound class destroyer
Built	White's, Cowes, Isle of Wight, 1943–4
Launched	April 1944
Commissioned	November 1944
Paid off	Chatham, 1972

SPECIFICATIONS

Displacement	1,710 tons (2,525-2,550 tons full load)
Length	110.57m (362¾ ft)
Breadth	10.87m (35⅔ ft)
Draught	3m (10 ft) mean, 5m (16 ft) max
Engines	Parsons geared turbines, 2 shafts. 40,000 ship horsepower giving 33 knots
Complement	186 (leader 222)

ARMAMENT

Four 4.5-inch guns
Four 40mm AA guns
Two to six 20mm or 2-pdr AA guns

HMS *Cavalier*, built by J. Samuel White of Cowes between February 1943 and November 1944, is the last surviving British destroyer from the Second World War. She was commissioned in time to take part in some of the Arctic convoys to Russia, and paid off at Chatham in 1972. As a steel ship she had scrap value, so when a charitable trust was set up under Vice-Admiral Sir Ian McIntosh, she was sold—not given—to them for about £65,000. This proved a great initial handicap.

On Trafalgar Day (21 October) 1977, the destroyer was towed to Southampton docks with Admiral of the Fleet Earl Mountbatten of Burma on board. Unlike HMS *Belfast*, she had not been stripped of much interesting equipment, but to renovate and preserve her some half a million pounds were required. She was not a great financial

Built in 1416-18, just after Agincourt, the lower hull of Henry V's great battleship *Grace Dieu* survives. *Photo: Alexander McKee*

success at Southampton, which is nowadays primarily a commercial port (although in Henry V's time it was a base for great carracks like the *Grace Dieu* which was burnt out when laid up in reserve in 1439—her remains can still be seen at low spring tides upriver from Bursledon). However, I am told that the main drawback to the Southampton site was that she appeared to be hidden away in an obscure part of the docks behind forbidding gates which looked as open and welcoming as the walls of Dartmoor Prison.

The destroyer was then towed eastwards along the coast to the new marina at Brighton, where she was berthed as near to the sea and as far away from the public as could be imagined. The berth was so exposed that the vessel might just as well have been serving at sea, with waves breaking over the wall and spray sweeping the decks: conditions which made upkeep costly and visitor-interest minimal. On any ordinary summer day, and particularly during the last few years, sunny Sussex probably has a Force 5 south-westerly for most of the time. True, there was a wonderful summer in 1976, but memories are fading.

When in 1987 I decided it was high time to visit the *Cavalier*, I learned that she had escaped me, having just been towed away again,

HMS *Cavalier* at her former berth at Brighton Marina. *Photo: Brighton Evening Argus*

to a destination in the north, somewhere in the area of Tyne and Wear. In fact she spent some months at a mooring on the River Wear, but a permanent mooring has now been found for her on the River Tyne, at Hebburn. When her future became doubtful in 1986, there was some uproar in the Portsmouth area, one ex-naval stalwart declaring that 'Portsmouth will continue to be the major centre of the world in its preservation of historic ships, attracting visitors from all parts of this country and abroad. If HMS *Cavalier*, one of the great class of fighting destroyers of World War II, were to be brought here, I would say that she would attract more visitors than HMS *Victory* and *Mary Rose*.' The proposition is arguable, but what is certainly not true is the belief that historic ships attract visitors from far and wide; foreign visitors, yes; but 'native' visitors, no—most come from the local catchment area. At the time of writing, South Tyneside Council have announced that HMS *Cavalier* will be refurbished by AMARC, a Manpower Services Commission scheme, before being opened to the public.

Enquiries to: Chief Executive's Office, South Tyneside Council, Town Hall, South Shields, Tyne and Wear. Telephone: (091) 455 4321.

The Experimental Launch *'Turbinia'*

SPECIFICATIONS

Hull	Built by Brown & Hood, 1893-4
Engines	1894, single radial flow steam-turbine 1895-6 onwards, three 'parallel flow' steam-turbines totalling 2,000 ihp at 2,200 rpm
Displacement	44$\frac{1}{2}$ tons
Length	30.48m (100 ft)
Beam	2.74m (9 ft)
Draught	1m (3 ft)
Maximum speed	34$\frac{1}{2}$ knots approx.

The ancestry of the steam turbine has been traced back to the Greek mathematician and inventor Hero, in the first century AD. The practical problems were to be solved in the late nineteenth century, not by the leading engine manufacturer but an Irish aristocrat, Charles Algernon Parsons.

After producing a successful turbine to power electricity generators for use in ships, he formed his own company at Heaton, near Newcastle, and then turned to the problem of using the same principle for ship propulsion, as an alternative to the reciprocating machinery used conventionally. *Turbinia* was built to be his test-bed. First experiments were disappointing, the launch reaching a maximum speed of 19.75 knots.

Parsons then built the world's first cavitation tunnel to study what actually happened when the screws revolved in water. After trying seven different designs and holding 31 sea trials, he fitted three turbines connected in series, with three propellers to each shaft. This proved much more efficient: in the 1897 trials *Turbinia* averaged 25.5 knots and for a time reached 31 knots. Parsons was now ready to demonstrate for maximum drama and publicity.

Queen Victoria's Diamond Jubilee naval review provided the stage—a mass of warships drawn up in lines and an immense number of spectators both at sea and on shore. *Turbinia* tore up and down the lines of ships at speeds of up to 34.5 knots—uncatchable by anything that floated. A picket boat sent out by the Navy to stop her interfering with serious matters was nearly sunk by her wash.

A passenger has described what some of the trials were like, particularly the 'citified garments' worn by the VIPs, in contrast to the heavy weather clothing of the crew. They had absolutely no idea

The *Turbinia* at full speed, demonstrating her capabilities during the Spithead Review in 1897. *Photo: Tyne and Wear Museums Service*

what was coming, so had to be enticed out of their velvet-collared overcoats and even top hats and into loaned overalls and oilskins. The *Turbinia* 'ran as smoothly as a bicycle on asphalt', working up towards 24 knots but still inside the river. Once in the open sea, the spray slashed back across the deck, speed was increased and an enormous wake began to form just astern, 'higher and higher, a greenish-blue tumbling mass, a solid mound of water with crest as high as the deck, tons of water swollen into a head that races after us like some angry monster.' Soon they were doing 40 mph.

The turbine was simpler, smaller and lighter than the gigantic reciprocating engines driving conventional ships, but there was still expert scepticism to overcome. However, under pressure from maritime rivalry with France and Germany, the Admiralty ordered larger-scale experiments: the two unfortunate destroyers *Cobra* and *Viper*, lost through no fault of the machinery. They were followed by HMS *Velox* (later to be a wartime casualty off Portsmouth)* and in 1906 by the decisive advance—the launching at Portsmouth of the

---

* *Velox* was discovered in 1969 and when I saw the wreck it was being stripped of all the copper and bronze which made it unique.

first 'all-big gun' battleship, HMS *Dreadnought*. She was powered by ten turbines. Cunard took the hint and their two new Atlantic liners, *Mauritania* and *Lusitania*, were fitted with turbines.

That became the pattern until quite recently, when the aircraft jet engine (suitably modified to work in a corrosive environment) was introduced into ships.

At the time of writing, the *Turbinia*'s future is uncertain. She is housed in a shed in Exhibition Park, near Tyne and Wear Museums' headquarters in Blandford Street, Newcastle-upon-Tyne. With the abolishing of the old metropolitan county of Tyne and Wear, her ownership is a matter for discussion between the district councils now managing the area's museums, and at present she can be viewed only by written appointment. Enquiries to: Tyne and Wear Museums, Blandford House, Blandford Street, Newcastle-upon-Tyne, NE1 4JA. Telephone: (091) 232 6789.

9 SCOTLAND

HMS *Unicorn*: A Frigate 'in Ordinary'

The *Unicorn* is a 150 ft-long 46-gun 5th Rate, or frigate, built to the lines of the French *Hébé*, captured in 1782. In many respects she is almost identical to the *Trincomalee* (see p. 39), Built of teak at Bombay in 1816–1817. The differences make her interesting, for the *Unicorn* came later, being built at Chatham, of oak, between February 1822 and March 1824, with structural changes devised by Sir Robert Seppings. After wooden ships have been at sea in all weathers for some time, the structure tends to work loose. To cope with this Seppings put in diagonal strengthening timbers, which have been claimed a revolutionary advance in warship construction. But this cannot be, for if you look at the recovered hull of the *Mary Rose*, whose last rebuild was in 1536, you will see that the same strengthening method has been employed in her.

Later, Seppings replaced wooden riders with wrought-iron pieces, and he also introduced in this ship what is claimed to be the first use of the same material, wrought-iron, to replace the enormous wooden brackets called 'knees', which had to be cut from naturally grown 'compass' timber. Replacing these with wrought-iron brackets saved much weight, and also 'compass' timber was growing scarce. But, alas, this claim also has been disproved by underwater discoveries. HMS *Invincible*, a captured French battleship of 1744, was wrecked off Portsmouth in 1758. Discovered by some of my friends some years ago, excavation has revealed iron knees.

Therefore it is with great trepidation that I repeat another long-established claim for Seppings (which, however, may well be true) that he introduced in HMS *Unicorn* the rounded stern. In both *Victory* and *Trincomalee* may be seen the old flat, transom stern (probably introduced by Henry VII in the fifteenth century, following a French example once again, because galleys could follow in the wake of a great carrack and shoot it up the stern with their heavy bow guns; and the answer to that was to construct a stern which would take two or more heavy guns to fire back). However, by Nelson's time certainly both bow and stern were very weakly built

HMS Unicorn at Dundee. Note the square stern and 'shed'. *Photo courtesy Unicorn Preservation Society*

above main deck level, and although guns were parked in the Admiral's and Captain's cabins which could fire back along the wake, both the front end and the back end of a warship were real weak spots for raking fire. As far as we know at present, it was Seppings who built them much stronger and made the stern semicircular instead of flat, to give a wider field of fire.

What is certainly true is that her state of preservation is far better than that of HMS *Trincomalee*, which would appear to contradict the statement that teak is a better material for shipbuilding than oak. But there were what may appear to us to be extraordinary circumstances affecting the career of the *Unicorn*. In 1824 there was no immediate employment for her, so that she never saw sea service of any kind. Instead she was put immediately into reserve, as a new hull which could be masted and rigged in the space of a few weeks, in emergency, whereas a hull could take the same number of years to construct. Therefore she was 'moth-balled' by contemporary methods—which meant constructing a roof over her to protect the hull. This was called putting the ship 'in ordinary', or reserve. And so she remained, first at Chatham and then, in 1873, at Dundee.

This was appropriate, for the first naval ship to carry her name was a galleasse of 240 tons, a flagship of the Scottish fleet, which was captured at Leith in 1544 and served in the Tudor Navy until 1555. In 1588 two quite different ships named *Unicorn* served against the Spanish Armada. The present vessel, now the third oldest ship afloat, spent the years from 1874 to 1968 as a naval training ship. In 1968 the Ministry of Defence handed her over, not merely for free but with a gift of £5,000 attached, to the Unicorn Preservation Society. When in 1972 she was docked for inspection, she was undocked two days later—because nothing very much needed doing.

To restore her fully as a rigged and armed ship was another matter, and this work has continued long since her official opening to the public, on a seasonal basis, in 1975. The main battery guns were 9 ft long 18-pounders, weighing more than two tons—replicas in glass fibre were made from an original weapon in Edinburgh Castle. Similarly, replicas of her 32-pdr carronades were made in the most authentic manner possible. The Carron Company of Falkirk, which in 1776 invented the carronade—a lightly-built short-range gun firing a heavy shot—also constructed the replicas. The originals could be devastating against wooden hulls because, whereas the swift-travelling cannon ball tended to make a small, clean hole in a hull, the slower, larger shot from a carronade tended to produce a rain of deadly flying splinters.

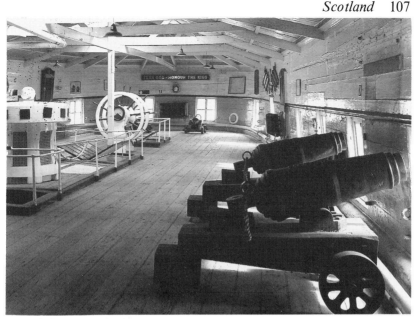

Gun-deck of the *Unicorn*. In the foreground are two 32-pdr carronades. *Photo courtesy Unicorn Preservation Society*

Although it is intended to bring *Unicorn* back to something like the state of a sea-going frigate of 1824, there remain interesting oddities of her almost century-long career as a training ship for the RNVR and RNR. For instance, large semi-circles in the deck at one point where a gunport has been enlarged, represent a pivot-mounting for a large breech-loading gun such as may be seen today on *Warrior*'s upper deck aft. What has been removed, alas, is a radar set—also at some time used for training.

Other historic mementoes include the four small brass guns by the entry port which are reputed to have been on board the flagship of the Scottish Admiral Duncan at his victory over the Dutch at Camperdown. He lived at Dundee and may well have carried them from ship to ship. Then there is the row of old wooden doors outside the Captain's cabin. These originally belonged to the *Duguay-Trouin* when she fired on the *Victory* at Trafalgar and were saved from a grave off Sussex when, as HMS *Implacable*, she was sent to the bottom in 1949.

There is a distant, historic link with the United States, for the *Leda*-class frigates, based on the French *Hébé*, included HMS *Shannon*, which captured the American super-frigate *Chesapeake* off Boston in 1813. The opportunity was taken to record the lines of the *Chesapeake*, before she was sold for breaking-up as building material. And, as building material, parts of the US frigate still survive in the structure of Chesapeake Mill at Wickham in Hampshire, only a short drive from Portsmouth Naval Base.

How to Get There
There is ample free parking on the quay beside the ship, which is berthed next to the Tay Road Bridge, only a few minutes walk from the City Centre. Map available.

Address
The Unicorn Preservation Society, Victoria Dock, Dundee DD1 3JA, Scotland. Telephone: (0382) 200900 Ext 209

Opening Times
1 April to mid-October: 10 am to 5 pm (4 pm on Sats).

Entrance Fees
Adults £1, 50p for OAPs, children, students, unemployed. Concessions for pre-arranged groups.

RRS *Discovery*: The Royal Research Ship

The RRS *Discovery* was the first British ship to be built for scientific exploration. She was laid down at the yard of the Dundee Shipbuilders' Company who had taken over the business of Stephen & Sons, specialists in wooden whaling ships designed to operate in the Arctic and, if necessary, to survive wintering in the ice field. This required not merely strength but cunning design of the hulls. Dundee, with its whaling fleets, was a leader in commercial exploration of the Arctic and its shipmasters had sailed further north than any one else. This aspect of the story has become lost in the tales of triumph and tragedy associated with the period of individual and nationalistic polar rivalry around the turn of the century.

It seemed then that the Poles, and particularly the terrible Antarctic continent with its storms frequently bringing down the temperature to minus 60°C during the winter, were the last unexplored areas on earth. But the year of 1901 was designated 'Antarctic Year' by an international body of geographers meeting in

Chesapeake Mill, Wickham, Hampshire—built from the timbers of the USS *Chesapeake* captured by HMS *Shannon* off Boston in 1813. *Photo: Alexander McKee*

1900. Three expeditions were despatched, the British one being a compromise between the views of the Royal Society (steady and systematic scientific exploration) and that of the Royal Geographical Society (a heroic naval expedition commanded by a dashing young officer). This was the enterprise for which *Discovery* was designed, now backed by the British government as a national venture.

The ship was designed for a loaded displacement of 1,620 tons on a 5m (16 ft) draught; overall length was 69m (226 ft), beam 10.4m (34 ft). She was barque-rigged with sails made from Dundee flax by Baxter Bros, and a triple-expansion steam engine from Gourlay Bros intended to give 450 hp, but which in fact gave 500. Double doors and skylights were fitted and thick lagging put in as insulation below the main deck. Provisions for two years could be stored, a steam-driven dynamo provided electric light, but the amount of coal which could be carried was limited to a few hundred tons, which was why she was basically a sailing ship, like the *Warrior*. Her steeply raked stem was 3.4m (11 ft) thick and designed to ride up over the ice and then, by its weight, break it, as the vessel slowly inched forward. The hull was 53cm (21 ins) thick and braced internally by massive crossbeams. The propeller and rudder could be raised into the hull if endangered by ice.

Discovery left Spithead in August 1901, and set out for the Antarctic from New Zealand in December. From 1902 to 1904 she was imprisoned in the ice. Some good exploratory work was done, in spite of the initial inexperience of most of those on board. The Admiralty sent out two Dundee vessels to rescue her, the *Terra Nova*, a whaler built by Alexander Stephen & Sons, and the *Morning*. They helped blast open a path through the melting ice and *Discovery* returned to England in September 1904. Her men had come the closest, so far, to the South Pole.

RRS *Discovery*, back in her home port of Dundee. HMS *Unicorn* is in the background. *Photo: Spanphoto, Dundee, courtesy Dundee Heritage Trust.*

Discovery herself was sold to the Hudson Bay Company the same year, and so was not available for Scott's final, and fatal, expedition of 1910–12. Instead Scott used the *Terra Nova*, built in 1884 as a whaler and not suitable for a big scientific expedition. 'Picked up second-hand in the wooden ship market, and faked up for the transport of ponies, dogs, motors . . .' wrote a member of that party. Amundsen, immensely experienced and not distracted by any scientific purpose, was first at the Pole from his specially-built ship the *Fram* of 800 tons. Scott's sledging party perished on their way back from the Pole more than a month later.

When, at the end of their sea careers, Scott's *Discovery* and Amundsen's *Fram* were in danger of the scrapyard, efforts were made to save them. The Norwegian campaign began in 1916 and triumphed in 1935 when the ship was hauled ashore at Oslo and a building erected about her. Smaller than *Discovery*, she seems very snug and comfortable. Scott's vessel was used by Sea Scouts between 1936 and 1939, and was then commissioned as a drill ship for the RNVR. In 1979 she passed into the care of the Maritime Trust and was opened to the public as part of an Historic Ship Collection in St Katherine's Dock, near HMS *Belfast*. The previous year a Gosport newsagent, one of many people who wanted to acquire her, had proposed bringing her to the Portsmouth area.

In 1985 the Maritime Trust, under its policy of chartering its ships to organisations which have the funds and also the physical resources, particularly dock and quayside space, to preserve and present them adequately, agreed with the Heritage Trust and the civic authorities that *Discovery* should return to Dundee, where she was built. On 27 March 1986 she left London for the Tay, where she is now open to view near HMS *Unicorn*.

Address
Dundee Heritage Trust, Maritime House, 26 East Dock Street, Dundee DD1 9HY, Scotland. Telephone: (0382) 25282

Opening Times
1 April to 1 June: Sat, Sun and Bank Holidays 11 am to 5 pm.
1 June to mid-October: 10 am to 5 pm every day.
Closed mid-October to April.

Entrance Fees
Adults £1.50, children 95p.

Scottish Maritime Museum, Irvine, Strathclyde

The Scottish Maritime Museum is at Irvine Harbour on the west coast of Scotland, south of the Clyde. It is a young museum, tentatively established in 1982, and is growing and changing. It is also a working museum, where you may see boat-builders, welders, riggers, painters and fitters at work on restoration and reproduction projects, and talk to researchers who can track down information on ships and boats and the people who built and sailed them.

There is an example on show of the diesel tug *Garnock*, built at Greenock in 1956 and presented to the Museum in 1984; she is both riveted and welded, showing the change in techniques (some restored ships have bumps stuck on to represent rivets, because the riveters' technique has been lost or is at least rare).

The RNLB *St Sybi* is an example of the big 52-ft Barnett-class lifeboats; this one was built in 1950 by J.S. White of Cowes, Isle of Wight. Placed at Holyhead in 1951, she saw 30 years' service around the rocky, treacherous Anglesey coast, during which she was launched 248 times and rescued 158 people. Relegated to the RNLI reserve fleet in 1980, she nevertheless launched a number of times and rescued another nine people, before being withdrawn from service in 1984.

Even longer service was given by the cargo ship *Kyles*, which was built on the Clyde in 1872, originally with sails to help her weak steam engine. She worked first on the Clyde with general cargoes, then in 1887 went to Newcastle-on-Tyne. By 1900 she was working on the Humber, out of Hull. In the 1920s she was a Cardiff-based dredger on the Severn and Avon. In 1942 she became a wartime salvage vessel, working out of Ilfracombe in Devon, but by the end of the war was employed as cargo vessel from Gloucester. By 1960 she was working as a tanker, dumping chemical waste far out to sea. In 1981 she retired to Cornwall, but came back to the Clyde under her own power in 1984, having circumnavigated the British Isles in more than one hundred years of continuous work.

Only a trifle younger is the Victorian racing gaff cutter *Vagrant*, built in 1884 by the Marquis of Ailsa's Culzean Ship & Boatbuilding Company, to a design by William Fife Jr. She spent her first century on the east coast of Ireland, during which time she was sailed as a cruising boat from 1929 to 1970 by Jack McGuinness, a one-legged veteran of the First World War. In 1985 she returned to Scotland to become part of the museum's fleet, and is regularly sailed from Irvine Harbour, a tribute to designer and builders.

The *Spartan* was built in 1942 as a humble servant of the Royal Navy of the type referred to as a 'puffer'. But her official designation was 'Victualling Inshore Craft Number Eighteen', so she was known as VIC 18. In peacetime she became *Spartan*, working the Clyde and out to the Western Isles, carrying bricks or coal and often beaching to unload cargoes at places which had no harbours. In 1961 she was

(*Above*) RNLB *St Sybi* on the slipway at Irvine, and (*below*) the Clyde cargo ship *Kyles* at Troon for survey. *Photos courtesy Scottish Maritime Museum*

(Left) the Victorian racing gaff cutter *Vagrant*, and *(right)* the old 'puffer' *Spartan*.
Photos courtesy Scottish Maritime Museum

given a diesel engine and later a steel wheelhouse and miniature modern funnel.

Address
Scottish Maritime Museum, Laird Forge Building, Gottries Road, Irvine, KA12 8QE. Telephone: (0294) 78283.

Opening Times
1 April to end October: 10 am to 5 pm every day.
Closed November to March.

Entrance Fees
Adults £1.50, children (three to 14), OAPs and the unemployed 75p.
Family ticket £3.00.
Groups by arrangement.

Merchant Schooner *Result*: The 'Q' Ship

In 1967 the Ulster Folk Museum and the Belfast Transport Museum amalgamated as the Ulster Folk and Transport Museum, based on Scandinavian open-air examples, on a 180-acre site at Cultra on the shores of Belfast Lough. The first galleries opened in 1976 and the museum is still being developed. The marine section is intended to represent various aspects of Irish seafaring, ship-building and boat-building, and already comprises some thirty-four vessels over a wide range of size and use. Some of these, such as the 357-ton sludge steamer *Divis* is still berthed in Belfast harbour. As a temporary measure, other vessels are still on a museum parking lot near the Transport Galleries.

Among them is the topsail schooner *Result*, built in 1892–3 at Carrickfergus Shipyard on the north shore of Belfast Lough. Three-masted and of 122 gross tonnage, she is the equivalent in steel of the *Kathleen & May*, now on display in London, representing the last of a line of traditional coasters. She carried cargoes until 1967 and in 1979, having been acquired by the museum, was lifted from the water at Harland & Wolff in Belfast Docks and then transported eight miles by road to Cultra, where visitors can watch her restoration. Measuring 37.2m (122 ft) long, with a beam of 6.6m (21 ft 7 ins) and 2.7m (9 ft 1 in) in depth, the move of the *Result* attracted much attention.

During her long career at sea the schooner was modified a number of times for different purposes, the most bizarre being as a 'Mystery' or 'Q' Ship to help combat the U-boat menace in 1917. Seemingly innocent cargo ships such as this—and a topsail schooner must have seemed particularly harmless—were equipped with buoyancy aids to keep them just afloat even if badly holed, and concealed guns and a naval crew. They set out to encourage U-boats to torpedo them and then, after the explosion of 300 lbs or so of warhead on their hulls, part of the surviving crew, forming a 'panic party', would abandon ship. Sometimes a parrot was carried, or a sailor, dressed up as the 'wife' of the ship's master, was among the motley-dressed

The schooner *Result*—HMS Q23. *Photo courtesy The Ulster Folk and Transport Museum, Cultra Manor, Holywood, Co Down*

crowd which rushed to a lifeboat. But as their stricken vessel obstinately refused to sink, the U-boat might surface and try to finish her off with a little cheap gunfire. All this time the British gun-crews would be lying flat on the deck, not moving or speaking, their guns disguised as hatchway covers, deck houses and so on.

The U-boat might take a cautious prowl round the 'Q' Ship, only her periscope showing, before her commander, deciding that the prey was harmless, gave the order to surface and begin a gun action. Then the wooden covers shrouding the concealed guns of the 'Q' Ship would fall flat, and the battle would begin. Serving as HMS Q23, the *Result* successfully decoyed U-45 and almost sank her; but her next opponent mounted a superior armament and it was HMS Q23 which was badly damaged.

One feels that, since this was the most exciting part of the schooner's long career, a 'Q' Ship replica might be made, showing how the decoy worked—and the very great risks run by her crew. As Admiral Bayly of the Maritime Trust has remarked, it is often cheaper to build a replica than to preserve a badly decayed vessel. The Ulster Museum find that although some of the boats they get are in good repair, generally they are acquired when their useful working lives are ended, so that much restoration and conservation work has to be carried out.

One example is the 10.4m (34 ft) fishing and passenger motor boat *Carpathia*, which was well worth repairing and restoring to original condition, because with her double-ended hull and clinker construction she was characteristic of many Irish workboats and hinted at a local Viking tradition of boat-building.

In 1973 an important addition to the collection was the *Mary Joseph* N 55, a 16m (52½ ft) decked, wooden fishing boat which had just concluded a working life of 96 years, beginning under sail only and finishing as a motor vessel. Although built at Kilkeel in 1877, her builder was a Cornishman and she is a traditional Cornish lugger of the type known as a 'nickey'.

Address
Ulster Folk and Transport Museum, Cultra Manor, Holywood, BT18 0EU, County Down, Northern Ireland.
Telephone: Belfast (0232) 428428

Opening Times
Mon to Sat 11 am to 5 pm, Sun 2 pm to 5 pm (October to April).
Mon to Sat 11 am to 6 pm, Sun 2 pm to 6 pm (May to September).
Open until 9 pm on Wednesdays during May and June.

Entrance Fees
Adults £1, children, OAPs and the unemployed 50p. Children under 5 free.
Group rates: Adults 50p, children 30p.

There is also an extension to the Museum at Whitham Road, Belfast, open Mon to Sat, 10 am to 5 pm.

Actually in Belfast docks, at Milewater Basin, is the light cruiser HMS *Caroline* (1913–14), which fought at the battle of Jutland in 1916. Since she is used by the RNR, however, she is not open to visitors.

APPENDIX 1

SHIPS HELD FOR PRESERVATION BY THE MARITIME TRUST, DECEMBER 1986

| | Total costs 31 December 1985 £ | Restoration expenditure during 1986 £ | Total costs at 31 December 1986 | | |
			Cost of acquisition £	costs £	Total £
Barnabas	20,638	–	1,200	19,438	20,638
Blossom	1,074	–	240	834	1,074
Cambria	11,214	–	7,000	4,214	11,214
Discovery	511,732	–	–	511,732	511,732
Elswick II	30	–	–	30	30
Gannet	52,088	3,861	–	55,949	55,949
Gipsy Moth IV	–	–	–	–	–
Ellen	5	–	–	5	5
Harbour Service Launch No 376	16,985	5,724	500	22,209	22,709
Kathleen & May	92,010	–	8,070	83,940	92,010
Kindly Light	4,806	–	4,000	806	4,806
Lively Lady	1,304	–	–	1,304	1,304
Lydia Eva	27,468	–	4,000	23,468	27,468
Peggy	265	–	200	65	265
Portwey	8,318	–	–	8,318	8,318
Provident	10,007	–	9,000	1,007	10,007
Robin	234,442	–	10,989	223,453	234,442
Softwing	9,798	–	900	8,898	9,798
Steam Cutter No 463	7,093	–	6,000	1,093	7,093
	1,009,277	9,585	£52,099	£966,763	1,018,862
Less: Amounts written off	1,009,277	9,585			1,018,862
	£ –	£ –			£ –

APPENDIX 2

VESSELS RESTORED BY THE MARITIME TRUST

Name	Type and date of build	Date of acquisition	Status
Barnabas	Cornish fishing lugger, 1881	March 1972	Sailed and maintained by Cornish Friends of the MT at Falmouth
Blossom	North East coast fishing mule, 1887	September 1971	On loan to Tyne & Wear Museums
Cambria	Thames spritsail barge, 1906	October 1970	Chartered to Dolphin Sailing Barge Museum, Sittingbourne, Kent
Cutty Sark	Tea clipper, 1869	January 1975	Open to the public at Greenwich (owned by the Cutty Sark Society)
Elswick II	Tyne wherry, late 1930s	September 1972	On loan to Tyne & Wear Museums
Gipsy Moth IV	Sir Francis Chichester's ketch, 1966	January 1973	Open to the public at Greenwich
Kathleen & May	Topsail schooner, 1900	June 1970	Open to the public at St Mary Overy Dock, London
Kindly Light	Bristol Channel pilot cutter, 1911	October 1971	On loan to National Museum of Wales, Cardiff
Lively Lady	Sir Alec Rose's ketch, 1948	May 1975	On loan to Portsmouth City Museums
Lydia Eva	East Coast steam herring drifter, 1930	May 1971	Laid up in West India Dock, London

Name	Type and date of build	Date of acquisition	Status
Peggy	Sunderland foyman's coble, 1890/1900	August 1972	On loan to Tyne & Wear Museums
Portwey	Twin screw steam tug, 1927	April 1982	Laid up in West India Dock, London
Provident	Brixham trawler, 1924	February 1971	Sailed by Island Cruising Club, Salcombe
Robin	Steam coaster, 1890	June 1974	Laid up in West India Dock, London
Softwing	Falmouth oyster dredger, 1910	July 1972	Sailed and maintained by Cornish Friends of MT, Falmouth

APPENDIX 3

VESSELS UNDER RESTORATION BY THE MARITIME TRUST

Name	Type and date of build	Date of acquisition	Status
Discovery	Royal Research Ship, 1901	April 1979	Chartered to Dundee Heritage Trust
Ellen	Gorran Haven crabber, c 1882	August 1972	Cornish Friends of the MT at Falmouth
Gannet	Auxiliary steam sloop, 1878	October 1971	Chartered to Chatham Historic Dockyard Trust
Hope	National 14ft dinghy No 1	June 1974	Isle of Wight
HSL(S) 376	Admiralty harbour service launch, 1944	October 1973	The Maritime Workshop, Gosport
Steam Cutter No 463	Tender to Royal Yacht, 1899	November 1974	The Maritime Workshop, Gosport

APPENDIX 4

MARITIME MUSEUMS, SHIP PRESERVATION ORGANISATIONS, OWNERS' AND ENTHUSIASTS' ORGANISATIONS
(Based mainly on information provided by the Maritime Trust)

Key:
MS   Museum ship open to public
M   Maritime Museum or Museum with maritime interest
S   Vessels in commission or organisers of sailing/steaming events
SP   Ship preservation organisations

M + MS	Aberdeen Maritime Museum	Provost Ross's House, Shiprow, Aberdeen, AB1 2BZ. (0224) 585788. Steam trawler *Explorer* (1955). (1955).
M	Admiral Blake Museum	Blake Street, Bridgwater, Somerset. (0278) 456127.
M	Arlington Court	Arlington, nr. Barnstaple, Devon. (0271) 82296. Collection of French POW ship models.
S	*Auld Reekie*	(VIC 27, 1943.) Working Clyde puffer based mainly at Oban, Argyll.
MS	HMS *Belfast*	Symons Wharf, Vine Lane, Tooley Street, London SE1 2JA. 01-407 6434. Now administered by the Imperial War Museum (qv).
M	Bembridge Maritime Museum	Bembridge, I.O.W. (0983) 872223. Models and wrecks.
MS	Black Country Museum	Tipton Road, Dudley, West Midlands DY1 4SQ. (021) 557 9643. Working boatyard and narrow boats.
MS	Blist Hill Open Air Museum	(Ironbridge Gorge Museum Trust), Coalport Road, Madeley, Telford, Shropshire. (0952) 586063. The Severn trow *Spry* (1894) and early iron canal tub boat.
M + MS	The Boat Museum	Dockyard Road, Ellesmere Port, South Wirral, L65 4EF. (051) 355 5017. Large collection of inland craft.
M	Botanic Gardens Museum	Churchtown, Southport, Merseyside PR9 7NB. (0704) 27547. Large dugouts and Galleries.
M	Bridewell Museum of Local Industries	Bridewell Alley, Norwich, NR2 1AQ. (0603) 611277, ext 299. Broads boats and wherries.
M + MS	Bristol Industrial Museum	Princes Wharf, Prince Street, Bristol, BS1 4RN. (0272) 299771. Steam tug *May* (1861).
M	Brixham Museum (British Fisheries)	Bolton Cross, Brixham, Devon, TQ5 8LZ. Also HM Coastguard National Museum. (0803) 557129.
M	Buckie Maritime Museum	Town House West, Cluny Place, Buckie, Banffshire, AB5 1HB. (0309) 73701.

M	Buckler's Hard Maritime Museum	Buckler's Hard, Hants. (059 063) 203.
M	Bude Historical and Folk Exhibition	The Old Forge, Lower Wharf, Bude, Cornwall. (0288) 3576.
M + MS	Caernarfon Maritime Museum	Victoria Dock, Caernarfon, Gwynedd. Preserved steam dredger *Seiont II*.
M	Cambridge Museum of Technology	Riverside, Newmarket Road, Cambridge. (0223) 68650. *Black Prince*, Fenland Barge, excavated 1974.
M	Captain Cook Birthplace Museum	Stewarts Park, Middlesbrough, Cleveland. (0642) 311211.
S	*Carrick*	Glasgow. RNVR club ship, formerly the composite sailing ship *City of Adelaide* (1864). Not open to the public.
SP + MS	HMS *Cavalier*	Chief Executive's Office, South Tyneside Council, Town Hall, South Shields, Tyne and Wear. (091) 455 4321.
M + SP	Chatham Historic Dockyard Trust	The Old Pay Office, Church Lane, Chatham Historic Dockyard, Chatham, Kent, ME4 4TQ. (0634) 812551. Restoring *Gannet*, displays artefacts from wreck HMS *Invincible*.
S	*Constable*	Quay Street, Sudbury, Suffolk. River Stour barge, 1820.
S	The Cornish Friends of the Maritime Trust	Sec.: John Trelease, 27 Duncannon Drive, Falmouth, Cornwall. This group looks after the Trust's Cornish vessels, lugger *Barnabas* and oyster dredger *Softwing*, sailing them on suitable occasions.
MS	Cotehele Quay	Cotehele, St. Dominick, Saltash, Cornwall. National Maritime Museum outstation and Tamar barge *Shamrock* (1899).
M	Cowes Maritime Museum	Beckford Road, Cowes, I.O.W., PO31 7SC. (0983) 293341.
M	The Cromer Museum	East Cottages, Tucker Street, Cromer, NR27 9HB. (0263) 513543.
SP + MS	The *Cutty Sark* Society	*Cutty Sark*, King William Walk, Greenwich, London SE10 9BL. 01-858 3445.
MS	RRS *Discovery*	Now owned by the Maritime Trust and under refit at Dundee by Dundee Industrial Heritage (to whom she is chartered), Maritime House, 26 East Dock Street, Dundee, DD1 9HY. (0382) 25282.
M + MS	Dolphin Yard Sailing Barge Museum	Crown Quay Lane, Sittingbourne, Kent. (0622) 62531.
MS	*Duchess of York*	1864 river steamer. Inn on the Beach, Seafront, Hayling Island. (0705) 468750.
S	East Coast Sail Trust	Jane Benham, MBE, 21 Butt Lane, Maldon, Essex, CM9 7HD. Own and operate two Thames sailing barges for sailing holidays for London children.
M + MS	East Kent Maritime Trust	Maritime Museum, The Clockhouse, Pier Yard, Royal Harbour, Ramsgate, Kent, CT11 8LS. (0843) 587765. Displays *Cervia*, *Sundowner*, *Vanessa*.
M +MS	Exeter Maritime Museum	The Haven, Exeter, Devon, EX2 8DT. (0392) 58075. Vessels from all over the world.

M + MS	Falmouth Maritime Museum	22 Market Street, Falmouth, Cornwall. (0326) 318107. Owns tug *St. Denys* (1929) a base for *Barnabas* (1881), *Ellen* (1882), *Softwing* (1910).
M + MS	Fisherman's Museum	Rock-a-Nore Road, Hastings, Sussex. (0424) 424 787.
M	Fleet Air Arm Museum	Royal Naval Air Station, Yeovilton, Somerset. (0935) 840565.
M	Fleetwood Museum	Dock Street, Fleetwood, Lancashire. (0772) 264062.
M	Fort Grey	Rocquaine Bay, St. Peter's, Guernsey. (0481) 65036. Ships and shipwreck museum.
SP	*Foudroyant* Trust	Frigate *Foudroyant*. 1817 frigate used for youth training. Under restoration at Hartlepool.
M	Furness Museum	Ramsden Square, Barrow-in-Furness, Cumbria. (0229) 20650.
SP	HMS *Gannet* (1878) Society	Chairman: David Muffett, 56 Maisemore Gardens, Emsworth, Hants. PO10 7JX. Local organisation of supporters of the *Gannet*, owned by the Maritime Trust (qv).
M	Glasgow Museum of Transport	Kelvin Hall, Glasgow. (041) 423 8000. Glasgow shipbuilders models.
S	*Gonola*	Steam launch, 1859. Regular trips on Lake Coniston. (0966) 58079.
M + MS	Grace Darling Museum	Radcliffe Road, Bamburgh, Northumberland, NE69 7AE. (066 84) 310. The coble used in rescues from the *Forfarshire*, 1838.
MS	SS *Great Britain* Project	SS *Great Britain*, Great Western Dock, Gas Ferry Road, Bristol, BS1 6TY. (0272) 260680.
M + MS	Gwynedd Maritime Museum	Porthmadog, Gwynedd. (The Ketch *Garlandstone* has moved to Morwellham.)
S	Hales Hall	Nr Norwich. A Norfolk Keel raised and under reconstruction. Not open to public.
M	Hartland Quay Museum	Near Bideford, Devon, EX3 96A. (023 74) 693.
M	Hartlepool Maritime Museum	Northgate, Hartlepool, Cleveland, TS24 0LP. (0429) 272814.
M	Hastings Fishermen's Museum	Rock-a-Nore Road, Hastings, East Sussex.
M	Hull: Town Docks Museum	Queen Victoria Square, Kingston-upon-Hull, HU1 3RA. (0482) 222737.
MS + S	Humber Keel & Sloop Preservation Society	Sec.: D. Robinson, 135 Waterside Road, Barton-on-Humber, South Humberside, DN18 5BD. Sloop *Amy Howson* and keel *Comrade* restored and sailing.
M	Imperial War Museum	Lambeth Road, London SE1 6HZ. 01-735 8922. See also HMS *Belfast*.
M	Institute of Maritime Archaeology	St. Salvator's College, University of St. Andrews, St. Andrews, Fife, KY16 9AJ. (0334) 4343 x 42.
S	*Irene*	Coasting ketch, 1907. Private Owner: Dr L. Morrish, Bishops Lodge, Oakley Green, Windsor, Berks. Not open to public.
S	Island Cruising Club	The Island, Salcombe, S. Devon, TQ8 8DR. (054 884) 3481. Sailing and cruising fleet including traditional yachts and Maritime Trust's Brixham trawler *Provident*.

MS	*Kathleen & May*	St. Mary Overy Dock, London, SE1 9DE. 01-403 3965. Schooner (1901).
MS + S	*Kingswear Castle* Excursions	The Signal Station, Chatham Historic Dockyard, Chatham, Kent, ME4 4TQ. (0634) 827648. Restored paddle steamer, passenger carrying in Medway area.
M	Lancaster Maritime Museum	Old Custom House, St. George's Quay, Lancaster. (0524) 64637.
S	Lightship	Riverside Road, Norwich. Owned by Sea Scouts. Not open to public.
MS	*Lincoln Castle*	Paddle steamer (1940) to be exhibited at Grimsby.
M	Lowestoft & East Suffolk Maritime Museum	Fisherman's Cottage, Sparrows Nest Park, Lowestoft, Suffolk. (0502) 61963. Models.
M	McLean Museum & Art Gallery	9 Union Street, West End, Greenock, Strathclyde, PA16 8JH. (0475) 23741.
S	*Maid of the Loch*	Balloch Pier, Balloch, Strathclyde. Paddle steamer (1953) used as a landing stage on Loch Lomond. Not open to public.
MS	Maldon	Maldon, Essex. Thames sailing barges in repair yards, and fishing smacks, steam tug *Brent* (1945).
S	Mariners International Club	Chairman: Erik Abranson, 58 Woodville Road, New Barnet, Herts. EN5 5EG. 01-440 9927. Members charter traditional sailing vessels for holidays.
M	Maritime Museum for East Anglia	Marine Parade, Great Yarmouth, Norfolk. (0493) 2267. Boats include early Broads yacht *Maria* and a Yarmouth beach boat.
SP	Maritime Preservation Society	Trevor Hughes, 37 Old Warblington Street, Old Portsmouth, Hants. Enthusiasts' pressure group.
SP + MS	The Maritime Trust	16 Ebury Street, London SW1W 0LH. 01-730 0096. The national organisation for preservation of historic British ships, founded 1969, now owns c. 20 vessels.
SP	The Maritime Workshop Ltd.	50 Ferrol Road, Gosport, Hants. PO12 4UG. (0705) 527805. Small boat restoration and building under youth training scheme, sponsored by the Martime Trust.
M	Marlipins Museum	High Street, Shoreham-by-Sea, Sussex. (07917) 62994.
M + MS	Maryport Maritime Museum	Shipping Brow, Maryport, West Cumbria, CA15 6AB. (0900) 3738. Steam yacht *Scharhorn*, a steam tug; a puffer and ketch *Emily Barratt* (1914).
MS	The *Mary Rose* Trust	College Road, HM Naval Base, Portsmouth, Hants. PO1 3LX. (0705) 750521. Wreck of the *Mary Rose*, raised in 1982, displayed in Portsmouth Dockyard.
MS	*Massey Shaw* & Marine Vessels Preservation Soc.	General Sec.: Mike Green, Kernow, 77 St. Albans Road, Seven Kings, Ilford, Essex. Members preserve and operate London fire float *Massey Shaw*.
MS	Medway Maritime Museum	Chatham Dockyard, tug *John H. Amos* (1931), tug *Tid 64*.
M + MS	Merseyside Maritime Museum	Pier Head, Liverpool, L3 1DN. 051-236 1492. Pilot Boat *Edmund Gardner* + 3 vessels not open to public.

M + MS	Morwellham Quay Recreation Centre	Morwellham, Nr. Tavistock, Devon, PL19 8JL. (0822) 832766.
S	*MTB 102*	Brundall near Norwich. Motor Torpedo Boat restored by Sea Scouts. Not open to public.
M + MS	Museum of London	London Wall, London EC2Y 5HN. Also promoting a Museum of Docklands in West India Dock. 01-600 3699.
M	Nairn Fishertown Museum	Laing Hall, Union Street, Nairn.
M	National Life-Boat Museum	Princes Wharf, Wapping Road, Bristol, BS1 4RN. (0272) 213389.
M	National Maritime Museum	Greenwich, London SE10 9NF. 01-858 4422. The national repository of maritime artefacts and archives. Paddle tug *Reliant* and reconstructions of North Formby, Sutton Hoo and Graveney boats.
M	Nelson Collection and Local History Centre	Priory Street, Monmouth, Gwent. (0600) 3519.
S + MS	Norfolk Wherry Trust	Sec.: Miss P.J. Oakes, 63 Whitehall Road, Norwich, Norfolk. Wherry *Albion* chartered for sailing on Norfolk Broads.
M	North Devon Maritime Museum	Odun House, Appledore, North Devon. (023 72) 4852.
S	Ocean Youth Club	The Bus Station, South Street, Gosport, Hants. PO12 1EP. (0705) 528421/2. Sail training organisation.
S	Old Gaffers Association	Sec.: W.A. Brown, Wheal Cock, Porkellis, Nr. Helston, Cornwall, TR13 0JS. Assoc. of owners of traditionally rigged sailing boats. Organise rallies and regattas.
S	*Olive*	Wherry yacht. Privately owned in Norfolk. Not open to public.
SP + S	Paddle Steamer Preservation Society	Sec.: J. Anderson, 17 Stockfield Close, Hazlemere, High Wycombe, Bucks. PS *Kingswear Castle* owned and restored by Society for passenger carrying, River Medway. See also PS *Waverley*.
M	Poole Maritime Museum	Paradise Street, Poole Quay, Poole, Dorset. (0202) 675151.
M	Portsmouth Naval Heritage Trust	College Road, HM Naval Base, Portsmouth, PO1 3LX. (0705) 839766.
M	Portsmouth Royal Naval Museum	HM Naval Base, Portsmouth, PO1 3LR. (0705) 822351 x 23868.
M	Royal Marines Museum	RM Barracks, Eastney, Southsea, PO4 9PY. (0705) 822351.
M	Royal Museum of Scotland	Chambers Street, Edinburgh, EH1 1JF. 031-223 7534. Collection of models including Dutch East Indiaman, 1719.
	Royal National Life-Boat Institution	West Quay Road, Poole, Dorset, BH15 1HZ. (0202) 71133. National (independent) life saving organisation.
M	Royal Naval Ordnance Museum	RN Armaments Depot, Priddy's Hard, Gosport, Hants. (restricted entry).
M + MS	Royal Navy Submarine Museum	HMS Dolphin, Gosport, Hants. (0705) 822351 x 41250. Submarines HMS *Alliance* and *Holland I* on show.

S	Sail Training Association	5 Mumby Road, Gosport, Hants. PO12 1AA. (0705) 586367. Operates sail training schooners *Malcolm Miller* and *Sir Winston Churchill*.
M	Science Museum	South Kensington, London SW7. 01-589 3456. National museum, including maritime items.
M + MS	Scottish Fisheries Museum	St. Ayles, Harbourhead, Anstruther, Fife, KY10 3AB. (0333) 310628. Includes restored fishing vessels.
M + MS	Scottish Maritime Museum Trust	Laird Forge Building, Gottries Road, Irvine, Ayrshire, KA12 8QE. (0294) 78283. Including Denny Ship Model Experiment Tank, Dumbarton.
	Scottish Veteran & Vintage Fishing Vessel Club	c/o Scottish Fisheries Museum, Anstruther. Assoc. of owners of pre-1940 vessels.
S	Sea Cadet Corps	Broadway House, The Broadway, London SW19. 01-540 8222. Sail training organisation (TS *Royalist*).
S + M	*SEONT II* Maritime Museum	Victoria Dock, Caernarfon, Gwynedd. (0248) 600835. 1938 steam dredger and ferry *Nantlys* (1920).
	Severn Warehouse Visitor Centre	The Wharfage, Ironbridge, Telford, Shropshire. (0952) 453522. Coracles.
M	Shetland Museum	Lower Hillhead, Lerwick, Shetland, ZE1 0LL. (0595) 5057.
SP	Ships Preservation Ltd.	The Custom House, Victoria Terrace, Hartlepool, Cleveland. (0429) 33051.
S	*Sir Walter Scott*	Paddle steamer on Lake Katrine. Enquiries: Strathclyde Water Department, 419 Balmare Road, Glasgow.
M	Southwold Museum	Bartholomews Green, Southwold, Suffolk.
S	Spurn Lightship	Hull Marina, Hull.
MS	St Katherine's Dock	London, E1 91B. Tug *Challenge*, Nore lightship, and misc. vessels.
S	Steam Boat Association of Great Britain	Sec.: Brian Smith, 19 Millbank, Kintbury, Berks. Assoc. of owners of steam boats, organise rallies, etc.
S	Steam Launch Restoration Group	Ferrol Road Yard, 50 Ferrol Road, Gosport, PO12 4UG. (0705) 586822. Look after a number of steam boats including two belonging to the Maritime Trust.
M	Stromness Museum	52 Alfred Street, Stromness, Orkney, KW16 3DF. (0856) 850025.
M	Sunderland Museum and Art Gallery	Borough Road, Sunderland, SR7 7PP. (0783) 41235. Models.
M + MS	Swansea Industrial and Maritime Museum	Museum Square, Maritime Quarter, Swansea, SA1 1SN. (0792) 50351. Steam tug *Canning* (1954), smack *Katie Ann* (1921), Helwick Lightship (1927), and Bristol Channel pilot cutter.
S	Thames Barge Sailing Club	c/o National Maritime Museum, Greenwich, London SE21. Organise sailing in traditional Thames barges, including own barges *Pudge* and *Centaur*.
M + MS	Tyne & Wear Museums	Blandford House, Blandford Street, Newcastle-upon-Tyne, NE1 4JA. (091) 232 6789. Two north east coast fishing vessels *Blossom* and *Peggy* are on loan from the Maritime Trust. Also Newcastle Science Museum and *Turbinia*.

M + MS	Ulster Folk & Transport Museum	Cultra Manor, Holywood, Co. Down, N. Ireland. (0232) 428428. Open air exhibits including steel schooner *Result*.
SP + MS	*Unicorn* Preservation Society	Frigate *Unicorn* (1824), Victoria Dock, Dundee, DD1 3JA. (0382) 200900 Ext 209.
M	Valhalla Maritime Museum	Tresco, Isles of Scilly, Cornwall. Collection of ships' figureheads. (0720) 22849.
S	*VIC 32*	Clyde puffer, 1943. Now holiday cruise ship: The Charge House, Crinan Ferry, Lochgilphead, Argyll. (0546) 5232.
MS	HMS *Victory*	HM Naval Base, Portsmouth, PO1 3PZ. (0705) 819604.
SP + MS	*Warrior* Preservation Trust	Victory Gate, HM Naval Base, Portsmouth, PO1 3LX. (0705) 291379. HMS *Warrior* (1860) on view to public at Portsmouth from July 1987.
	Warrior Association	Sec.: John Cooper, 18 Leventhorpe Court, Elmhurst Road, Gosport, PO12 1NX. Supporters for HMS *Warrior* (1860) in the Portsmouth area.
M + MS	Waterways Museum	Stoke Bruerne, Nr. Towcaster, Northants. (0604) 862229.
S	*Waverley* Steam Navigation Co. Ltd.	Anderston Quay, Glasgow. 041-221 8152. Operate the last sea-going paddle steamer in the world, PS *Waverley*, on passenger cruises throughout Great Britain.
M + MS	Welsh Industrial & Maritime Museum	Bute Street, Cardiff, CF1 6AN. (0222) 481919. Bristol Channel Pilot Cutter *Kindly Light* on loan from the Maritime Trust.
M + MS	Whitehaven Museum and Art Gallery	Market Place, Whitehaven, Cumbria, CA28 7JG. (0946) 3111, Ext 307. Steam dredger *Clearway* (1927) in Whitehaven harbour.
M	Whitby Museum	Pannett Park, Whitby, YO21 1RE. (0947) 602908.
S	*William McCann*	Hull sailing trawler, mainly based at Bristol.
M + MS	Windermere Steamboat Museum	Rayrigg Road, Windermere, Cumbria. (096 62) 5565. Collection of steamboats on display and in steam.
S	*Windsor Belle*	Restored Thames excursion steamer. Enquiries: c/o 17 Boswell Road, Henley-on-Thames, Oxfordshire.
M	Wool House Museum	Bugle Street, Southampton. (0703) 23941. Medieval Warehouse. Liner models. May add waterfront premises with space for small vessels.
SP	World Ship Trust	Sec.: Major J.A. Forsythe, Scoutbush, 129a North Street, Burwell, Cambs. CB5 0BB. (0638) 741612. Launched 1980 to campaign for ship preservation at international level. Publish an international register of historic ships.
M + MS	The *Zetland* Museum	King Street, Redcar, Cleveland. (0649) 371921. *Zetland* (oldest lifeboat) on display.

NOTE: Appendix 1 is correct to December 1986, Appendix 2 to December 1987, Appendix 3 to December 1987, and Appendix 4 to January 1988. Developments, changes and alterations (especially as to opening times and entrance fees) are certain to occur. Anyone planning a visit to any of the ships and museums listed above is strongly advised to check by telephone or letter beforehand. For example, in the past Portsmouth Naval Base has sometimes been closed on security grounds or for VIP visits.